This book is to be returned on or before
the last date stamped below

E1/19
15 FEB 2019
-7 JUN 2019
02 01/20

Taug... et-
wise ...ty
profe ...th
his te ...h.
Quie... de
chara...

WITHDRAWN

East Lothian
Council

FOREWORD.

 For those of you, like me, who grew up in the rural environment of the West of Scotland, life was always that bit rough and ready. When, for example, a man and two boys went out foxing two fields from away some friends decided to terrorize them on departure. I was sixteen at the time and having two older brothers this always made me the youngest of the biker gang that congregated at our house, or, as I always felt the one left behind.
 As the trio departed in a small car, in pursuit was a posse of motorcycles overtaking, undertaking, pulling wheelies and in general just making a nuisance of themselves. Years later I had the good fortune to work beside one of those two boys so felt obliged, somewhat embarrassed, to apologize for past actions. I tried to explain these were my friends, this was my home but I had no control over what went on. David was a decent lad who just shrugged it off for he had been neither frightened nor offended by the experience and said the driver was also a biker who had done similar antics in his youth. Later on he admitted the three of them were not out foxing but had a dope plantation up on the hillside. Christ! I was sixteen and thought I knew how a dirty world turned but there was a cannabis plantation in my back-yard yet I didn't even know it existed!

 After that experience I didn't want to know what was going down anymore. Human nature is a strange beast, where the more I ignored events the more I found out what was really happening. People are inclined to inform you of criminal deeds if you have no interest in the subject, compared to someone constantly asking questions. Back then we all shared a common enemy – the police. In particular one policeman offended us more than any other, this was PC H. Having said that, I secretly preferred him to any other; I always thought differently about situations. In the face of universal hatred because of the way in which he victimized the whole neighborhood, friends and particularly my eldest brother, I harbored reservations about the subject. I could foresee someday the PC Hs of this world with their big shiny *Doc Marten* boots would be replaced by a younger, thinner, meaner, cockier, more intelligent breed to eradicate the old school – the future looked bleak. From then on, life was destined to take a sinister turn. To give you an honest insight of what I am trying to portray it is best summed up in another short story.

At nineteen, I was in town visiting a friend to find him alone at his bedroom window armed with an air rifle, or as they were known to us at the time a slug gun. The barrel protruding out the window with him engrossed in picking off all the wildlife in the adjacent gardens. At a knock on the front door he handed me the gun with a warning not to shoot one remaining sparrow on the telephone line in front of a neighbor's house further up the street. This was sound advice; the small bird was distant with the neighbor's window directly behind the target where risk of missing and shooting out the glass was too great. Guns and killing never excited me contrary to what most people thought, but this shot did. Temptation was too much. I took aim, did the mental calculations with the distance and side winds estimating how much the projectile would drop over that distance, raised the gun barrel to a full inch above the bird's head, then knowing not to pull the trigger squeezed it gently to watch in amazement. The sparrow trilled 180 degrees on the wire then plummeted straight down, head first, in a majestic fashion. The perfect shot, the perfect kill, as I stood up full of euphoria feeling like a junior version of Carlos the Jackal. I had never even held that rifle before but could take on such a shot and be successful!

An unusual formal, "Robert" a shout came down the stairs, "The police are looking for you."

Oh shit!

Their efficiency that day appeared to be breathtaking. I laid down the gun not knowing what he had previously shot-up but knew I was the one who would have to take the fall for all his past misdemeanors having been the last person left holding the offending weapon, plus not being in the know regarding how I/he were caught. Ashen faced I came down the stairs thinking, 'Say very little; say yes sir, no sir'.

All along this mate had been in conversation with two policemen. To my relief it was the scourge of the neighborhood, PC H, accompanied with a younger colleague. PC H was always loud and liked to hear the sound of his own voice, when asking in a domineering fashion, "Is that your car, Son?"

"What car?" I cunningly asked going outside dragging them away from the house and the scene of any potential serious crime still unsure to the relevance of all this.

"The *Saab*?"

A polite, "Yes, it's my father's car."

"It's parked on a flower-bed," the officer retorted upon being a keen gardener.

This was a gross exaggeration. The car was parked upon a grass verge separating the pavement from the road. PC H operated in a confrontational manner; others would have been offended at him calling them 'Son' in case there was a remote possibility of being related to him, or pointed out there was no flowers in his so called flower-bed – not I. Instead of dwelling on these points that could be contentious, it was time for a wind-up. Here, for the second time in five minutes temptation again over-whelmed...

What I would do was put the words into his mouth to watch him shout them straight back again, but there was one major fault with this strategy because after a period I would burst out laughing, therefore I knew to keep the exchange brief. Mischief making began with, "I should know better Mr. H."

To be followed by a predicted, "You should know better Mr. Rae," boomed in high decibels. From there the exchange continued in this manner; me thinking up an appropriate sentence only to hear it being loudly returned with one or two words exchanged. The man never realized nobody made a greater fool out of him but he never once charged me with anything. It would have been possible to get him to say he molested donkeys if I'd given it enough thought when behaving in this manner! Two golden rules were never annoy him and don't argue with him, otherwise you could commit any crime to never be caught. Had others fathomed this out they could become master criminals without a single charge against them. There was also the classic case of me giving PC H an *idiot test* one day. He passed or failed in splendid fashion depending on your point of view, but someone ended up in prison so it is best I don't reveal what I did that time.

Policing was changing, crime was changing, and the world was changing around us from those early days of *innocence*. I found the reflection of this in the son of PC H not paying for a bag of golf balls I sold him at school. Sometimes we were in the same class together but he never paid nor did he have any intention of paying. He was after all a policeman's son. In the village in which I went to primary school three brothers joined the force, two in uniform with the other going undercover. The son of the eldest brother ordered Chinese meals when I was delivering one night, where on payment the money was all counted out but deliberately short of what it should be only to be told sarcastically to, "Keep the change."
I knew what he was doing when it happened, therefore walked away without challenging him, but only thinking sarcastically, 'You'll go far if you follow in your father's profession.'

The new breed, the next generation of policemen, they were epitomized for me by the behavior of that obnoxious boy. One-day, we might all lament the phasing out of policemen like PC H!

1. HARD LESSONS

'*At that point there was three of us there, myself, another lad and the owner of the house who was a gangster, but we took little notice with him sitting there with a calendar and telephone counting out the weeks then disagreeing with his arithmetic. Finally he announced, "No; it is next week I grass myself in."*
I was young and bright, or maybe that was only in my youthful estimation, therefore offered the advice, "I don't think you want to do that."
This lad was sharp; he also had a sense of humor repeating these words with an addition, "You don't want to do that, you might give the judge a heart-attack."
"What are you talking about? Give the judge a heart-attack?" asked the geezer.
The lad explained that it was not every day a judge got to jail someone for two hundred years, if he did indeed decide to grass himself in for his crimes, probably giving the judge a heart-

attack in the process. He protested with, "Yous don't understand."
To be answered, "I don't think we do."
From there, he went on to explain he was self-employed and every year when the tax-woman came calling he was in prison for a couple of weeks at the exact time for her to assume this was a long term prisoner therefore didn't have to submit tax forms. How could he; when his income from his activities did not correspond with what little legitimate work was carried out. He was planning to receive another small sentence again. I was nineteen at the time and had just learned a valuable lesson on how to beat the system.'

Gateside Primary School was like something out of an Amish village, where it was here I first went to school. Two elder brothers preceded me, who had not been popular, so when I turned up I could instantly feel animosity from the teachers and, in particular, by the headmistress. From that initial frosty reception I felt condemned at birth. Only, unlike these brothers I was highly intelligent, so not all the few teachers we got detested me, where in general I was treated fairly. One teacher, who I unfortunately can no longer name, always displayed great warmth and affection towards this incredibly clever little boy over the brief period she taught there. As a young man I would see her in the town near the village in which we'd been together years earlier. Even with the passage of time, she hadn't changed her appearance and was always alone, no boyfriend or husband, nor did I see her in the company of other women, and sometimes we'd look at each other in a puzzled manner. I now shared great affection towards her but was too quiet and shy in my early adulthood to introduce myself so never said who I was. Maybe it was the loneliness more than past warmth that made these feeling prevalent.

My class was large for this rural school; there were nine of us in the year, two girls and seven boys. We were repeatedly reminded by the teachers we were the most notorious class this small school ever had, where out of the nine, five pupils were considered bad. I was included in this group, not that I was particularly disruptive, solely because of my brothers' lack of popularity. This was the archaic manner in which it operated. I was once belted (given four lashes of the leather strap on the hands) for flushing twin brothers' heads down the toilet. These boys were classmates. I never did such a thing nor contemplated doing such an act, but you couldn't protest, where you just had to keep quiet and accept your punishment – that's how it was. The attitude was, *'Shut up, or just think what you will get if you were to do something wrong'*.

At the end of the seventh year there was a shield to be won by the pupil who scored the most marks from English and arithmetic tests combined. I scored the best but they gave the trophy to another classmate. Not only did I feel cheated but to add insult to injury they gave *my* trophy to a girl; the lowest form of creature on the planet or so I thought as an eleven-year-old. For once I overcame my quietness to find the gumption to stick a hand in the air and say, "Please Miss."

The teacher, who had recently married causing her some difficulties with being called *Miss*, asked, "What is it, Robert?"

I complained, "I won that shield, I had the most marks."

She was completely beat for an answer standing there humming and hawing for a few minutes, then finally answering after long delay, "Yes, you did have, but we worked it out as percentages."

This was one clever kid who was not deceived by that answer knowing I also had the highest percentage. At the time I considered sticking a hand in the air for a second attempt to say words to this effect, only I was too shy and ran the risk of being belted if I did, therefore refrained. However, I did win a prize for best hand-writing. How strange, at times I struggled to read the scrawl that passed for my hand-writing!

It is easy to slate Gateside Primary for all its quirks and quaintness but the education standard from this rural school was probably the highest in Scotland, irrespective of the discipline and how it was administered?! You go to school for an education and that place certainly educated me - about life. I was now eleven years old, I'd suffered seven years of unjust persecution to be cheated at the outset. Gone was any inclination to ever receive an academic education again. When I went to the *big* school I would just be another face in the crowd, which suited me for I could sandbag my way through secondary education and never come to anyone's attention. Once it was all over I could breathe a sigh of relief and put the whole rotten experience behind me forever.

Of the disobedient five classmates, two quickly settled down to family life on leaving school, where the other two chose a life of crime, stealing cars, before retiring then settling down. I am the last, I am still out there, only now am I succumbing to the grow-up, grow old, get married, raise rug-rats then die routine. Otherwise, the class all remained friends well into adult life such was the close bond between us with the exception of that one girl, which is quite ironic given what happened.

Secondary education was at Garnock Academy, where it catered for three towns plus a host of small villages. Up until then it was standard practice to place the few pupils from Gateside in one class instead of separating them alphabetically by surname like they did with kids from the other larger primary schools. Only, the nine of us were too unruly so had to be split up, as were classes from Gateside after ours. Garnock was a volatile mix of pupils, which was found out when the school first opened its doors with school-children from the neighboring towns fighting each other, rioting with weapons five hundred on either side. I arrived to witness the end of this practice with numbers reduced to fifty per side; bottles stones and bricks being hurled at each other, and then the insults, before one side would charge the other and they would all run never actually engaging in battle. Outside school, they continued to fight when Beith Juniors played Kilbirnie Ladeside at soccer or at the annual event of Beith Fair. The only rumpus I was involved in was in third year in the English corridor. This was when the other two classes came to fight with our joint classes. We were going to stand our ground and fight unlike those first riots witnessed upon arrival. Our group lost that fight - convincingly - but it was obvious we'd put up a gallant defense with the entire corridor left in darkness afterward because electric fuses had blown such was the damage done to the interior of the building. Plasterboard walls in the corridor had holes kicked and punched in them where blows had went astray and electric sockets were smashed – some of which were done after as a mark of belonging. On a personal front, I could not have been beaten-up as badly as most of my classmates were because when the teachers went to pick out those involved this was done in the next class attended by recognizing torn clothing, cuts and bruises, and fresh blood. I sat there quietly watching half the boys in the class being dragged away amid protests of, "No Sir, I burst my nose when I fell down the stairs," "Riot; what riot?" and, "It wasn't me Miss, I got this black eye when I tripped over in the playground; honest!"

Truth be told, we lost so badly because our class was a victim of its own policy. Our class had a dwindling population because only two new male pupils ever survived the initiation service. Jimmy was from Glasgow where initiation went on with regular beatings for years. I resented the cruelty meted so offered him advice on how to stop this punishment, "The first one that comes at you, break his nose, forget the rest, just hit the first one, put him in hospital, he will never attack you again."

Poor Jimmy, he never heeded this, replying, "No, I couldn't do that."

I even offered to fight with him on the one condition he actually did stand and fight instead of just cowering up for protection, but again he flatly refused.

Years later I found out he was more terrified of his mother than he was of those frequent beatings therefore could not ask to be moved out of our dreadful class in case she found out. Could the woman not see the marks on her son's body and ask what was happening to him? Did she have no compassion for her son? Jimmy, on leaving, joined the British Army; I dread to think what a sadistic bastard he became because of the abuse inflicted from school. He was a cheeky boy at times but there was no justification for the punishment received.

The only other new male recruit our class received was Mark. He was South African. His family was originally Scottish who returned when trouble brewed there. A giant compared to new undernourished classmates, with the build of a man, square shoulders set off with a pleasant personality. Rules were rules, so as part of his initiation service he would have to be downed, but the only thing was, with four fourteen-year-olds upon his broad shoulders and others attacking him from the ground he still never hit the floor. What were we going to do?

There were three arenas for our fights, understandably the playground, the PE (physical education) halls and interestingly the music class. It had not always been this way. When we went to music class we were too troublesome to be trusted with musical instruments, although some of the quieter pupils did go missing during lessons with the suspicion they actually got to see some brass. To the rest of us such an object would only be used as a weapon. I personally never once got to touch a musical instrument. This may be hard to believe, but because of another of our antics we also got singing lessons banned at times. Instead of singing what we were supposed to as a choir, a favorite ploy of a select few was to sing a *Sex Pistols'* song at the same time. The teacher playing the piano would listen to something confused that went like:

*'Nick knack paddy whack give the dog a bone,
This old man came rolling home,
He stuffed his ass with broken glass,
And circumcised the skipper.'*

Alarmed at what she'd just heard, she would suddenly look around missing keys on the piano with the tune now resembling a punk number much to our delight. Due to embarrassment, fear of corrupting the few polite pupils present and an inability to catch them responsible, singing was also not allowed at times. We were in a class that could offer nothing in the way of education. Boredom set in. Once again we became victims of our own policy – would we ever learn?

To alleviate this state of affairs we invariably started fights. Mark had been in our class for months now and still he'd never been initiated. That day a determined bunch of us would *have* him during a music lesson! This was it, this time, there would be no mistake was what those junior thugs promised each other gleefully.

The music teacher opened the classroom door, looked at what was going on, screamed and ran down the corridor in horror; she witnessed an initiation service! Her timing had been poor where upon opening the door to see two chairs in mid-flight bounce off the indestructible Mark, a group of young tear-aways, undaunted by her presence, with chairs above their heads swinging and hitting the South African about the body and others grappling with him. It never started this way. Five youths attacked him but he never fell over so out of frustration chairs were thrown and thrust at him as a last resort, but the unfortunate teacher witnessed the worst of the violence.

We were read the riot act and threatened with everything this side of death for this incident, but this meant nothing to us compared to the battering our pride had taken: Mark, although now with tears in eyes, to his credit had never been toppled and he wasn't even Scottish - in our opinion! I was in further difficulties when I offered to fix one of the many broken chairs but instead lay underneath it in the same manner a mechanic would when repairing a car and said, "I think it is the spark plugs, could you pass me a spanner?"

It was in the other boxing ring of the changing room of the PE halls where I had my greatest victory. Boys from two classes would be in the same room together, which inevitably ended in violence. Out of a sense of order someone fool-heartedly suggested we should have organized fights for once instead of our usual free-for-all. A bold suggestion beset with a major problem, nobody wanted to be on display fighting in this manner. Finally, Beefy stood up then approached, saying, "I'll fight with Chubby."

Chubby was my nickname, where Beefy had been picking on me for weeks, with the occasional kick and punch here and there that I by and large ignored. I was expecting this so thought, 'Do you?' in a manner that belied an underhand confidence.

Over he came and started slapping and punching me about the head but I was still seated trying to tie laces for circuit training we were about to do as a class. Then I muttered lowly, "Let me finish."

In my defense someone shouted, "Let him get up."

Not even addressing me by my name for it was a foregone conclusion due to the size difference between us I would be beaten - severely. Beefy conformed to the request to step backwards. His first mistake I deviously thought to myself with a smirk concealed on a bowed down head, securing laces then getting up. Quietness descended all around due to what was viewed as a slaughter with my bravery-cum-stupidity because the best way to avoid this situation is to remain seated, and so we met in the middle of the floor for the spectacle; him being the biggest and most feared and me the smallest but also feared. The class of over thirty boys all seated around the four walls initially never made a sound when they watched in amazement realizing I could not only take his pounding but returned it punch-for-punch. Then he made his second mistake. A small half step backwards. This was what I was waiting for when he went onto his back heel. Bang! Bang! Bang! Upping the tempo hitting him fast and furious. He ran for the door not even throwing punches anymore but I was, raining fists down on him like the sails of a windmill, as five classmates leapt to their feet to try and restrain me. How could they do this? He'd been picking on me for weeks then wanted to humiliate me in front of the whole class yet there they were rescuing him! I sat down again smiling, both satisfied with my handiwork but frustrated, thinking, 'Is there no justice in this world?'

This incident had two effects. He intentionally kicked me in the face two weeks later and claimed it was an accident. Riled, I got up off the ground to swing a hay-maker of a punch at him but missed; he was after all a farmer's son. My middle brother witnessed the incident intervened and prevented me from *killing* him.

The other incident arose from my, couldn't care less, attitude. At the school the Kilbirnie boys all stood in the doorway in the middle of Technical Block. These were the hard men of the school (or maybe that was only in their estimation). My mates used the doors at the end of the building to avoid confrontations with them. Not me. If these were the nearest doors I just trundled through them being kicked punched and spat on in the process. After the fight in the PE halls, walking up to the doors they frequented, I could hear "That's him. That's Chubby. That's him there. Here he comes."

For once, even I was starting to have reservations about this situation. For the sake of ten extra paces I could avoid all this aggravation by going to the other doors, but it was too late now. I was too close. When I got to the point where I believed I would lose my front teeth a strange thing happened, they parted, jumping out of my way and even held the door open for me. I walked through them feeling like royalty turning my head from side to side in an upwards manner, squinting up at them in disbelief. Inside the building I started to laugh at the fact all these comparative giants were afraid of, or respected me, thanks to the incident with Beefy.

For a final word on the situation; the two of us had grown up together and went through Gateside Primary together; what did you expect!

Of all those Kilbirnie boys there was Rab. A brute of a boy credited with being the best fighter in the school, but I threw an ice-pole into the crowd one day that hit him of all people! The school bell rang as he came over where I never before or after seen my classmates disappear so quickly to their classes. Back then, he appeared to be about three times the size of me but too full of his own importance to actually inflict some damage grunting an arrogant, "Do you know who I am?"

Two years after leaving school I was standing alone at the bus-stop when he came along again with an enormous swagger, but it was only for the fact there was two of them did I stand back to avoid a confrontation. He didn't appear any taller or heavier from when he was at school, but I had grown and I was now in superman shape where I knew I could beat him. Time plus having been so small as a kid distorted proportions for me. Fighting is psychological, where if you know you can win, you inevitably can. When I had been downcast and written off as a nutcase for getting to my feet to fight with Beefy that day the only person to know I was going to win was me. Little did they know I had made myself a vow that I would lose body parts first – it never came to pass.

At college, as a nineteen-year-old, I was to prove such superman condition. David was in my class, we were of the same size and build, where he was competing for the British Power Lifting title, which meant daily training and strict diet. Our class held a mock contest to lift a 28lb weight with two straight arms where he unsurprisingly could manage the best by holding the weight up for over twenty seconds, until I came along and only put my left hand on it. The chorus of, 'Fuck off, Rab' went quiet when I held that weight up for over ten seconds with one arm. I always like to keep something in reserve, whereas if I had used my right arm it was possible to better twenty seconds.

As for the other Rab from the school days, I ran him home one night because he was short of money for a taxi but never said who I was; it was all in the past now. Even doing so in knowledge of a mate claiming this was now a police informer!

Garnock academically was not the best, where in third year they separate you according to ability in arithmetic mathematics and English classes. Our year was one of the biggest ever, and here was I in the second bottom mathematics class with this being a deliberate result of my under-achieving policy because of experiences at primary school. The class below me was for the real retards, them that, 'their mothers had dropped them on their heads when they were babies.' Thankfully, I escaped that class with accompanying stigma. At the first assessment test the class average was around 24 percent, I in contrast to others scored a record 84 percent and knew I had completely overblown it to be caught out sandbagging in the most dramatic fashion. The class was taught at a slower pace of learning whence it was impossible to get over 70 percent, but here was someone with a ridiculous result well in excess! Think of an excuse quick in case they question you on the matter, was how I thought. 'It must be a fault in the education system,' sounded about right.

I never needed to explain this record result; for this, after all, was the big school where students become nameless and faceless. I was moved up immediately into the second top class. Fortunately I was spared the top where pupils go on to become bank managers and accountants. I didn't want to be like that or associated with this type of pupil though I was extremely quiet and intelligent. The future was looking bleak at this point, I was thirteen and thinking up ideas such as getting a snake tattooed onto my face so I could never become a bank manager. It was obvious I'd came to the attention of the school authorities when asked to explain not this but another sandbagging technique; going into the third year you get to choose what subjects you wish to study but with constraints like compulsory subjects plus an overview to take a broad range of topics. On examination, there was found to be no science subjects on my schedule nor did I have any languages. What was it to me, an 'A' pass in an easy subject like art was as good as an 'A' pass in any other subject, but they never seen it that way. As for the overall education system, you only needed to be clever for the hour when they have the final test in the various subjects to pass the 'O' grades or Highers. I was, and knew it, so this is how I operated in passing. Swats could study for years on end and still fail, but having never studied, I, on the other hand, couldn't fail and didn't.

The glorious day came after five years when I got to leave that awful place striding out into the sunshine as a sixteen-year-old with some girl calling after me from an upstairs window. I turned around for the last time to blow her a kiss unable to see clearly who it was, then was gone forever. It was always meant to be this way, walking out into the sun like the end of a romantic movie. This life had never been bought out of a catalogue, instead I was living the Bruce Springsteen song *'Born to Run'* that was a favorite. Friends mostly left after four years or less, but I had been too young to leave then, which got me down. I survived the experience with only one visible scar, I was wanted by the police for attempted murder and had some impressive qualifications to top it off. Educational wise I could count read and write, plus I discovered that I possess a real talent for technical drawing so Garnock Academy wasn't all bad. Only once did I score below seventy percent for technical drawing; that being for the Higher to receive a 'B' pass instead of an expected 'A'. Maybe I was paying the price for my lazy behavior at the end of it all. Unsurprisingly, I had also learnt how to fight and knew how to evade the law. Further, by then life had already given me my first tentative lessons in politics and terrorism. What more could a budding juvenile outlaw ask for?

A scar visible on the back of my hand was received in woodwork class. A sharp chisel went astray just after being warned by the teacher; not to do that. My thumb opened up diamond shaped like a blackbird's mouth where I looked down to see over an inch of white rod I now identify as bone, set against a red background. Unbeknown then a tendon was severed. This had cause for a visit to the family doctor who was surprised at my appearance. Instead of repairing the wound, Dr. Hibbard, who I knew from outside the surgery, produced the folder that should contain personal medical records, opened it up and waved it about upside down but nothing fell out.

"How did you do it, Robert?" he asked. "All we have on you is a name. You have never even had the standard jags. You have completely beat the system."

I stood there thinking systems are there *for the beating*, but if I wanted to see a clown the next time I will go to the circus. Could he not just attend to the injury and send me on my way?

I had on one occasion before this seen medics obviously unknown to Hibbard. My mother got a new washing machine where my eldest brother asked me to go inside the cardboard box it came rapped in so he could play a game; he proceeded to hit the cardboard wrapping with a hammer. I went off to hospital afterwards with a warning from my parents, "Don't tell the nurses your brother hit you over the head with a hammer."

I never understood what his game was, for there was no humor in it for me, nor did I understand what I was supposed to tell the medical staff. I was just too young at the time. Was I meant to say I had been eating a hard-boiled egg where now half of it is stuck to my head?

How I escaped not having another scar on the other hand defied reason. Maybe this complemented the art of generally not getting caught. It was during a power-cut myself and Ross went looking for fire-alarms to break so the fire-bell would ring when the electricity was reconnected. Ross found one he wanted broken but then announced we should return later to smash it, at which, I refused, so punched it on the spot only to have the broken glass cut the back of my hand. The two of us then spent the next class out behind the dining block with some girls, all sunning ourselves on conveniently placed sitting room chairs. With one of the group playing at nurse-maid attending the injury, it was looking rather contentious when the assistant head-teacher appeared and caught us. Mr. Paterson rounded on me in particular because it was his class I had been caught skipping. I knew my bacon was fried this time, for there was nobody more senior with teaching duties. The bloody hand would reveal who smashed the alarm, if he were to see it, and I would then be looking at criminal charges along with school discipline procedure. With the injured arm dangling at the side of the chair so the blood could secretly disappear into the grass, when he said angrily I was for the 'high jump' I graciously accepted this thinking, 'And, you're telling me!' He then left, presumably so I'd follow him back to class. How could I, as he would then undoubtedly see the blood to then have me charged with destruction of school property. In this situation I couldn't have been more caught yet reprieved!

I did, however, have another scar from the schooling but it was concealed. One afternoon four of us decided to *dog the school* (play truant). On walking down from Todd's corner shop on the broad pavement I was on the outside about eight to ten inches from the edge when something hit me a glancing blow on the side of the head. I spun round like a ballet dancer on my left foot not knowing the cause. A lorry mirror was the culprit where the vehicle stopped at the bottom of the hill. Out of embarrassment I suggested to the others, "Let's give the driver a good kicking."

As we walked down to our prey Allan said, "Your head's split open!"

We were always fooling around where I wasn't going to be caught out here, so dismissed it with, "Fuck off."

Either Gordon or Alan confirmed this in a trembling voice, with, "It is."

At this I could feel something that felt like a large insect on the back of my neck so put a hand back to grab it. Upon opening the fist again in front of my face instead of any crumpled creature being there there was a surprise handful of blood. The lorry driver never got the beating he deserved, but not missing the trick I used him as a taxi service to get to the doctor's surgery.

The National Health Service (NHS) provides free medical care for most people, which culminates in the fault of surgeries being full of people who need not be there. For many women it can be a social club. On entering Kilbirnie surgery this was the case with one present about to see the doctor with little or no ailment, when I walked in, leaving a trail of blood... Three other women about to be attended to would soon have genuine reason to see a doctor now that a psychopath was sitting amongst them. What did these people have wrong with them? One looked if she'd a mild common cold that there is no remedy for. Another, as if she'd found an extra freckle on a breast, with the third still trying to think up a reason for being there, as she counted her fingers relating to times past she used whatever different excuse for attending the practice when being healthy. Unbeknown, I was about to fill her need when a soft voice enquired, "What happened to you, Son?"

With the pool of blood on the floor getting ever larger with every drop from my head (it looked more dramatic than it was), I snarled, "I got hit by a lorry!"

At this all three with visions of a school-kid being mangled by a truck conjured up images of a horrific situation where all began to shudder with varying degrees of shock. She, without an ailment, could now stagger through the doctor's door to be assessed for something exotic like post-traumatic-shock-syndrome or post-traumatic-stress-disorder. They should be grateful I appeared that day to alleviate them of their boredom even if I deliberately never finished the sentence: I got hit by a lorry 'mirror'.

The situation was shown up for what it was when the call came to see the next patient. One of the trio said in a trembling voice, "You can go next, Son."

At this I surveyed them in a searching manner. Fragile nods of the head all round in agreement. Inside the surgery the doctor cut some hair then stitched the wound with butterfly stitches that were more painful than the actual injury, to then send me on my way.

I know you shouldn't do it, but I once did a wind-up in a hospital one day, long after the above experience. Ten men and ten women lay up and down the same ward where I was the first to be doctored when the nurse asked me to roll onto a side and then jagged a left buttock with the needle of a syringe. I was bored, so instead of rolling back again I never did but let some saliva trickle out the side of my mouth and started muttering incoherently to the terror of the other patients, as they watched in horror thinking, 'They're not going to do that to me; they're not going to turn me into a zombie like they did to him!'

People can be so gullible because the jag administered never had time to take effect when I started acting up. The doctor knew what had happened therefore treated me harshly afterwards for terrifying her other more sensible patients.

You may be wondering why the police wanted me for attempted murder before I ever left school, but it was not at sixteen, it was for an incident as a fifteen-years-old. A friend came round when it was snowing and so as pillion on his motorcycle we raced up the single-track road over the hill towards the neighbors' house. In a blizzard, the two of them were in the middle of the road. The motorcycle had a poor headlight. When narrowly missing one all that could be seen were the feet of the other as he dived into the ditch. We never hit him. The incident was an accident and their stupidity could be questioned, but because of it the police wanted to charge the two of us with attempted murder. Police arrived at our house (a standard practice then) with motorcycle tracks visible in the snow confirming who was responsible because they led to and from the shed, but they left, and then my mother telephoned around the countryside telling the two of us not to come home. Maybe the police were also starting to get pissed off with this little English neighbor who phoned them too regularly with her complaints. Those were the days when you slept beside an open window, even in wintertime, so you could jump out it in the middle of the night. At school the next day, when asked what I had been up to the night before the answer was 'attempted murder'. That would give those unruly classmates something to better...

The actual case of attempted murder I was about to commit was when a wind-up by four mates on myself all went wrong when they staged a break-in on the family home at 3 O' clock in the morning. Two older brothers were also present that night but all they could do was shit themselves whereas I was a different proposition. At the time they remained upstairs when I went downstairs alone, as they whispered down there were five men outside breaking into the shed, miscounting the strangers in the night. I had a need to, so armed myself with an axe and small hammer. When one of those five came past the front door his shadow became exaggerated in the moonlight to make him appear about seven-feet tall. At which, I became scared so hid behind the hall-stand adjacent to the front door with the axe above my head waiting for whoever it was to come through the door to execute them medieval style. I personally didn't care who entered the house that night – parents, for example, returning from holiday – I was going to split them in two then decide what next... The situation never materialized but a motorcycle started and sped out of the shed. At this, a brother read my nature correctly when whispering down again, "Chubby, don't go out."

Famous last words! I forgot my inhibitions, ripped open the front door, and then ran up the road barefooted hatchet and hammer in hand to attack the perpetrators. On approach to the car, what I couldn't understand was why the engine never started to run over the top of me especially so when the headlights were switched on to illuminate the situation. Upon realizing the small hammer was in my left-hand, with which I would have a poor throw to stick it through the car windscreen, therefore I refrained and so kept hold of it. In this situation it was imperative to keep the axe to fight the supposed five men with, whereas a small hammer was an irrelevance that could be handily disposed of. Right at the driver's door with the axe about to cleave the driver's head in two, like the two halves of a chocolate Easter egg, there was laughing. It was a friend Kevan, and soon afterwards three others made themselves apparent. Needless to say, they were never brave enough to wind me up again in such a fashion. I was sixteen then and the smallest and youngest of the group, but somehow believed this is how you behave in these situations. I had that kill or be killed mentality from a young age, where on this occasion I had gone out that night to die, not to win or evade but just to fight to the bitter end, in a last-man-standing is the winner scenario! When you start believing you can triumph in these situations is the day they wrap you up in a straight-jacket, this I have always been certain of.

This may have been the first time my attitude towards fighting, life and death, became apparent to the public but certainly it was not the last time I would demonstrate this frame of mind – it held me in good stead for future events... Unbeknown then, a life of brutality would soon materialize.

[In those teenage years it had probably always been exceptionally wild, it was just that back then everything was so fast and crazy it never registered, and having never known any different this was what I considered the norm.]

Margaret Thatcher's Britain was already a topic of conversation before I even left school. Where, upon, arguing with a friend, Derek, about the miners' strike, stating, "They will never win."
He protested with, "What, you are arguing against men fighting for their jobs?"
Derek, proudly wore his *'Solidarity'* badge, took this the wrong way. Solidarity was the Polish trade union that was later influential in bringing about the downfall of Communism. For I knew Thatcher was not going to be beat by striking miners and blatantly told him so – sadly enough this proved correct. My argument was not about the ethics of men fighting to save their jobs and industry, but it was purely being realistic about the Conservative Government's stance. The position was they never gave an inch to anybody or anything. This impossible way of reasoning and what transpired from it, did however provide my first lesson in terrorism. Before that came to fruition, at school one science teacher, who had come over from Northern Ireland, readily told pupils how to make *good* fire-bombs, but I never heeded his advice. Although, I would look somewhat bemusedly at, '*Your Country Needs You!*' wartime posters he'd just forged, and wonder if it all came from a grudge against British society in general. Was he out to fuck the entire system educating impressionable delinquent teenagers in this manner?

When I joined a group of friends one evening racing motorcycles around a field beside a busy main road, they would stop with the shout, "Here comes the coal lorries."
Coal lorries in question were a convoy of armored trucks transporting loads of coal around the country designed to break the miners' strike with orders not to stop for anything because the drivers would most likely be attacked by angry protesters. I watched in fascination when this group left their bikes, picked up stones and lined the hedge beside the road then threw their missiles into the path of the approaching protected vehicles.

Some took direct hits. Those youngsters responsible held no interest in politics, industrial action, Arthur Scargill, Margaret Thatcher or downtrodden miners; it was just an opportunist act of terrorism with no concern for the other road users or the lorry drivers' safety.

Hindsight is a great thing; one of them responsible, John Danks, was ironically killed in a road crash later on. The local policeman, PC H, who we hated so vehemently in our youth, warned us this would be the outcome, but we were young and wild thinking we were invincible so naturally never took heed. It was on a raid of our shed, when I was asked to explain how I managed to own three motorcycles at the age of fifteen, PC H declared, "I've scraped nineteen bodies off the road so far."

Were we going to listen to someone who on leaving addressed my father with, "Your sons are not criminals Mr. Rae; just daft."?

Of course not, but his insight and experience proved correct to our detriment. Even without his insults it is doubtful we would listen to any policeman, for that would be viewed as capitulation. Of all my many friends and cousins who died young, they practically all died in road traffic incidents.

[For the record; the last I heard of PC H, he is now retired but remained one of the few policemen I would actually casually talk with, not that we particularly liked each other now. It was just a mutual understanding between us – bygones be bygones.]

So these were my schooldays; I left school fully educated but questions lingered about motives regarding certain aspects of schooling. These queries didn't matter where it was the big bad world now... This was the west of Scotland at the time of what the Scots Irish Welsh and many English referred to as 'Thatcher's reign of terror'. To the south of where I lived coalmines were closing, to the north shipyards were shutting shop, and east and west the steel industry was being dealt its death knell. By this age, I no longer believed in democracy, protests were pointless, school-mate Derek being a case and point, police were not to be trusted, and, if I wanted a job the advice was go to London. It was like a child being born into an African famine. Such a set of manifestly corrupt circumstances is sole destroying for young people about to make their way in the world, not that the Tories in London acknowledged it or wanted to, or catered for the unfortunate. I did, surprisingly, find work unlike most, but resented paying taxes to what I viewed as a foreign dictatorship. We were Scots and our money made London rich was how I seen it. After working twenty-three months I found myself unemployed because if I completed another month (two years) that would entitle me to employment rights. However, this was Thatcher's Britain, a land of exploitation and greed where I learnt I'd become another victim. At the time, unbeknown to me, I was doing an apprenticeship. This came about when I was asked to give a second signature to documents when working in that factory. Being young and naive, I didn't know the company deliberately had me sign these papers for my benefit, incognito, such were their devious ways.

On British soil I would never take another legitimate job but of course there were many offers. I unfortunately (in these circumstances) ended up with a reputation and talent for many different professions therefore was offered all different kinds of work.

There he was offering employment; the job title was a *'Real Gem Cunt'* and this one of life's more colorful characters. What can I say; cunt, as most people know, is slang for part of a woman's anatomy but gem comes from the Scots language. Where if you are gem you are up for anything, do anything. This potential employer continued, "Five guys come at you; you are unarmed; you will go ahead with the five of them?"

I started to answer, "Yes, I have done it in the past, but ..."

To be abruptly cut off with, "I know you have, I know your past."

Of course this was so, it was the only reason I was still alive talking to him that day but what I failed to explain, or denied opportunity to explain, was I couldn't do it for money. Rare times I had went out and committed an heroic act I accepted I was dead anyway and had just went out to finish off my life in a blaze of glory. Ironically it was this crazy attitude that kept me alive for all these fraught years!

This was not something you could put on a CV: -

1. Cabinet-maker.
2. Real Gem Cunt.
3. Van Driver.

Somehow a future employer might just pick up upon it, start asking questions about what was really going on for all those missing years. Half the time it would be easier to explain the past by saying I was locked up in prison, but I never received a custodial sentence. There are difficulties filling in the gaps on the CV, but I always tried to keep my work legal (within my framework) other than a little tax evasion.

That's how it really was. Despair was rife, unemployment rates high, so we were destined to become part of, 'Thatcher's wasted generations', and I resolutely remained certain I was never going to fight the corrupt system. I found such a proposition completely pointless; fight against Thatcher, you must be joking. Those television pictures of boot-boy policemen assaulting miners remained fresh in the mind. These were desperate men struggling to feed their families coming home with blood on their clothes after the protests. Images were complemented with a Government orientated propaganda campaign to demonize the miners' leaders. Anyway, that was the politicians' job, but the Scots voted Labour and their fifty Scottish MPs were dubbed the 'feeble fifty' by the Scottish National Party (SNP) because they refused to rock the boat. Labour members knew sooner or later they would be returned to power therefore didn't want to be too harsh on the current Government in case the tables were turned when they came to govern later on. That's politics for you. In the meantime the Scottish nation would suffer any abuse the ruling classes wanted to inflict upon it. Not that it ever changed under the Labour Government. My plan was just like the one devised for secondary school; keep quiet, no one will notice you then get the results at the end-up when it is too late for anyone to see what you have really been up to. Only, life is a tougher proposition to fool than some poor school authorities.

As for family life, my father gave up on me at fourteen, not that he particularly bothered a button before that. It was just that I could remember the actual incident. Gypsies came around one night wanting my motorbike. It wasn't running right at the time, so what the hell, they were the ones wanting it so I swapped them for an old pick-up truck. There, with Beefy as co-driver, I received a first driving lesson when he complacently said, "Put your foot to the floor and ask questions later."

I did. We were on a twisted single-track road with high embankments that guided the vehicle as it bounced off one side to another at high velocity. A two-position throttle was reduced to one-position when the accelerator cable broke for we tied the throttle full open. There was nothing like it at that age, a vehicle that was completely out of control with two maniacs at the helm who had a stop-when-you-hit-something attitude – if that were possible now! Later on my father came to the front door with the engine roaring outside, headlights shining into the kitchen. Shaking his head in despair he retreated closing the door for safety. The two of us were sweating and laughing at the same time, for we were both stinking of petrol we'd just siphoned out of his car to put in our new mode of transport.

My mother was different; she never seemed to give up on me, which became a bit over-bearing at times as an adult. In all fairness, she always made my company welcome even when they were considered undesirable by others. Such is summed up in the words of a brother's mate, "No matter who you've raped and murdered, you would still get a bowl of soup at your door."

The woman held Christian values without the pretentiousness that usually accompany them.

Although both are my parents, they came from a different era, a different background to the one I found myself in. At times I questioned their naivety. God knows what they question about me; I gave them plenty of scope!

Well, there you have it, the complete picture. I may have grown up with a certain amount of crime and violence but as these things go it always looked worst from the outside, whereas all it gave me was a greater acceptance and more balanced outlook on society. To be in such a situation doesn't make you a bad person;

it just gives them that way inclined an opportunity to vent their anger. In Scotland, Paisley is the biggest town and close to where I lived. In the nineteen-eighties, it had a higher murder rate than the city of Belfast, but there was no politics attached just good old-fashioned violence. Back then; this town was probably the most violent place in Europe. For amusement as teenagers we would drive there at night just to watch the fights. The older I got the more I came to reject violence completely but sometimes it is inescapable, sometimes it is forced upon you, sometimes it is the only answer. As for politics and fighting against the oppression, I had defeatism engrained in me from an early age like many other Scots such was Thatcher's reign of terror (and before Thatcher it was probably the same), but at least I could see right through the Labour Party with the pretense of the feeble fifty. Negativity from the overall scenario prevailed well into adult life. As one of the most down-trodden races of people in Europe, but unable to stand up for ourselves, what a pathetic bunch Scots really are.

In all the madness, where in the past reminiscing on it, all I could do was laugh such were the crazy situations but in present times this is no longer the case. As youngsters we lived, we had metaphorically pissed against the side of a moving bus, can kids now-a-days claim the same or are they too wasted on drugs or stuck to computer screens never knowing what to be alive really means? It is a difficult scenario for others to grasp, where all that transpired resulted from me being, in most instances, the smallest and youngest of the group, be it family or friends. In many situations I believed I was the last line of defense. You couldn't turn to the police when you felt they created more crime than they ever solved and their only purpose was to victimize members of society solely to demonstrate the terror of an evil regime. Such a syndrome is irrespective of getting a reputation for being a grass if you were to with the alienation that accumulates, or the risk of increasing the victimization. There was nowhere to run, nowhere to hide, nobody to turn to, big brother wasn't going to stick-up for me and my father never concerned himself. It was the other way around, where I didn't get to bullshit like others, so the buck stopped here whenever it really mattered. There were no soft options here, no quarter asked or given, I would have to do it the hard way every time. To know the rule book didn't apply to anyone in authority such was the inherently corrupt society I was never going to conform with the hypocrisy of it either. From which I always preserved one thing more than any other, a sense of justice – probably because I was always denied it. The biggest misunderstanding of them all was I had been brought up to be law-abiding where by the age of sixteen I had all but ran out of rules to break!

This education and upbringing was preparation for something, obviously different from routine, but what? Storm clouds were gathering over the hills of the west of Scotland…

'The innocent and the beautiful have no enemy but time.'

2. A CASE STUDY.

'At the farm situated over the hill from where I lived some friends were bored one day so started a gun-battle – with each other. Thankfully, I was not there as two of them ended up with serious injuries. How could you ever explain such an event to ordinary people?'

This live evolved in seven year cycles. At seven-years-old this was the best days and the spin-off from them. The sun always seemed to be shining back then, like it does when you are a child. When as children we roamed the countryside carefree like it was our kingdom. Then at fourteen I took depression and continued to be haunted by it in the future. It never left me in adult life, although abated somewhat latterly. At twenty-one I survived a serious car crash that should have killed me (the prophetic words of the detested PC H proved correct once again much to my annoyance) and suffered many years of agony henceforth. Back then, *in the wild days*, we predicted we were never going to see twenty-one. This wish was nearly granted was it not for the fact I was in superb physical condition I should never have survived. That night I lost a drinking contest with the driver then came close to dying when he embedded the vehicle into a cemented stone garden wall at forty-five miles-per-hour. Speedometer was said to have been jammed there with the force of the collision indicating the speed at the moment of impact. After this crash I developed something that was never an over-riding concern before; fear! I would also never be so physically fit again. At twenty-eight began a life of torment - more on that one later. Then at the grand old age of thirty-five apprehensive in regards to what will happen. I shouldn't have been having already suffered the depression, pain and torment, what else is there for life to throw at me? Either marriage, failing health or old age for a probable answer?! My age is disputed upon possessing a younger look, where I confess it was all too messed up to even know if my documents are genuine or not. In the past I was offered a new passport from the mob therefore remained uncertain if I had bought my identity in the back of the pub. Temptation prevails to sell the present passport to someone I don't like because I regularly get arrested when crossing British borders. Depending upon the political situation at home at the time (more accurately, how scandalous it is in relation to what they have to cover up), I find myself arrested with regularity elsewhere in the world. This is the interference from the British authorities.

The actual answer to what would happen at thirty-five came in the guise of the SAS…

The year was 1997 and I was twenty-eight-years-old, this was the start of years of torment. Rumors circulated MI5 rated me the most dangerous man in Britain, which I felt was a very awkward title. It was back to that feeling of thinking you've really done it this time. Even by my standards, where I have a habit of overdoing it at times, this was completely overboard. So many people would have craved that one, killed for it, but not me, especially so when I just wanted to blend into the background. I was too small, too shy, too introverted to hold such a title; so what was it really all about when I only ever claimed to have saved many lives? Maybe I had got caught out sandbagging again, but this time with life. The only certainty was I could never live up to the prominence achieved if it was for conventional reasons. However, if the claimed status were true the motives behind it had to be out of the ordinary. Only something like that would be fitting with my personality. When your life becomes this messed up it becomes a comedy – a bad one. Few people, out with a wartime situation, ever get to know that I'll be dead in the morning anyway scenario. What it does is it alters your perception on daily life to the extent you cannot return to a mundane existence. You become crazed; you become the psychopath looking for the next battle. Where damningly you live for it, entice it, look for the greatest threat then go challenge it… Ultimately, in outright paradox, a regular existence in these circumstances will only get you killed?!

In that year the Provisional IRA were at full strength with numbers of volunteers and arsenal at their disposal. Never before could any Irish Republican Army boast of having so much firepower. They had hundreds of active volunteers, thousands of past or dormant members, tens of thousands of supporters and worldwide the number who favored them ran into millions. Their infrastructure spanned the globe and was said to be as competent as any multinational organization. Could they not make The Slab, the alleged leader, the most dangerous? Much to his annoyance, he partially lives on disputed British soil. His farm straddles the North/South Irish border. At some point in time he obviously held this title.

Then in the following year a settlement to appease most of the violence in the Province of Ulster was agreed. Under the Government of Thatcher, there was speculation about redefining the Northern Irish/Irish border so that The Slab and other members in the vicinity could be placed inside the Republic. This was rejected because the border would have to be moved nearer Belfast, likewise the perceived threat coming closer with it upon surrendering territory, which could upset the political apple-cart too much for British tastes; i.e. a small defeat.

London crime had also been hit by a new phenomenon by this time; this was the Adams family. Three brothers from a large family who were sometimes dubbed the New Krays after the notorious Kray twins that ruled the London underworld in the nineteen-sixties. These brothers came to my attention, and that of others, after a gun-battle on the streets where they used small sub-machine-guns to fight rivals. Their influence came right down the valley in which I lived; allegedly.

Finally, in 1997 there was Johnny Adair; one of the best-known Loyalist terrorists since Gusty Spence started the concept. By accident or design, or as these things go probably both, he'd become something of a celebrity from The Troubles of Northern Ireland. Someone like that constantly featured in the media could revel in my title. I would gladly give it to him but it wasn't for me to allocate. It was a burden I certainly didn't want. Loyalist terrorists now, by this year, had a more refined operation compared to predecessors. Further, they were now accused of less collusion with the security forces operating there, therefore deemed more secretive, likewise hostile, in the eyes of the British authorities – though this could just be a ruse to deflect suspicion from outright Government agent involvement?!

Of these five men countless offenses could be attributed but I surpassed them for unknown reasons. You couldn't be a charlatan in such company claiming something you are not; these were not the type of people you wanted to offend. In Scotland, I was head and shoulders number one. Number two listed was the most prolific hit-man the country had known for a long time. I knew who he was, where he was from and what he looked like; with good reason, living every day with a contract out on my life, but this was not who was supposed to execute me. This hit-man remained out of the league of them that deployed my would-be executioner. As for my actual stalker-cum-killer, he would drive past my home on a regular basis in his dark car, occasionally drink in the same pub, trying to find a pattern in my movements so he could set me up for the kill (Special Branch and MI5 likewise, but I never received an Osman Notice, where they only see what they want to see?!). He shouldn't have bothered because knowing where he lived when in the vicinity I made a habit of driving down his street. I don't honestly know why I did this, to annoy him, to piss him off I suppose. Maybe it was a ploy to catch him off balance and make him look like the amateur he probably is, or it could simply be curiosity. Corresponding with this, I just had a bad attitude towards him, call yourself a gangster, that type of thing, step this way and I'll show you what a real geezer looks like... What appeared on the surface to be a *Fight Club* mentality was not, for I always did what was least expected to the constant surprise of others. This practice was purely about survival, where it worked in the past and probably would be a successful means of defense in the future. When all else failed, at times I would describe a prevailing situation to an unconnected individual and ask how they would deal with it, then go and do the total opposite so not to be predictable. Security forces use psychological profiling to anticipate their target's future movements. Would they, or others who were after me, anticipate mine when behaving like this where I was asking a different person each time for their slant on matters? This worked well until I asked a notorious relation his opinion on a certain situation. His answer surpassed even my most outrageous antics... As for the actual contract out on my life, there was no hiding place when it really came to it. This in the west of Scotland where there is only one law, the law of the jungle, which is survival of the fittest (or maybe there is a second with Police and Intelligence agents being a law unto themselves as demonstrated?!). I would just have to fight him where one of us would most likely end up in the bone-yard. A lack of sincerity could be put down to the fact all I really needed to know was when he was approaching so I could give him a welcoming party. Maybe it was boredom that made me behave in this manner, where I needed the adrenaline rush of being on the edge one last time. Like an old boxer, it is always that one last time, as he makes many a comeback. The truth is I didn't take him too seriously because the Men in Black already tried to murder me but they were, for once, unsuccessful. At the end of the day it only takes one bullet to kill you irrespective if I never rated him with his local reputation as a gunman or the half-witted morons that put out the contract. I can still see their moronic faces with saliva running down their dirty chins complete with an allergy they shared to a bar of soap.

Unsurprisingly I knew the basics about firearms such as capacity and range, and how to survive a gun attack, like not choosing a shotgun to fight the Men in Black with such is its lack of killing potential in a human context. I held the fear of humiliation, where they would only laugh at me before the execution if I was holding such a weapon. For another example, when this hit-man appeared to finish me off, there was no sense in running from him even if I was unarmed. No; what you do when you are looking at the end of a gun barrel where he has his finger on the trigger is to grab it, pulling the gun sharply towards you so it does fire but deflecting the discharge away from your body in doing so. With the gun then unloading when removed from the gunman's shoulder, thereby recoiling into his ribs, I am told this has the potential to actually kill the gunman by shattering his ribcage, but I have yet to meet anyone who has actually done such a trick to verify this technique. The process described only works with high caliber firearms. An example of this was when I gave a friend a shotgun to fire where she nearly end up on her back such was the kick it gave, especially so with her having no experience with firearms therefore oblivious to the impact of the recoil and with her being so petite.

You have a six weeks lifespan at the top of the most dangerous tree, but I was fortunate to come off the top without the prison sentence, hospital bed or a visit to *Auld Nick's Ceilidh* (fires of hell). Plenty of attempts were made to give me one of the three, or at times it looked like they were going for the treble but still couldn't hit the target. In the end they gave *my* title, two years later, to Richard Baker. Notoriety obviously enhanced here by the fact I could elude them for so long. They probably got frustrated chasing me round in circles - where I intentionally did this - without anything resembling a positive result. Whereas the lovable Richard, or Dick for short, was a serial rapist who avoided detection by operating mainly in Spain on young female British tourists who were less inclined to report attacks to Spanish police. Once caught, he went down for thirty-five years. On getting out he will be hard pushed to raise a smile never mind an erection. They probably gave him the title just to annoy me when struggling so hard to dispose of who they feared most.
'What you gave my title to a pervert; how could you do such a thing?' Those nice chaps at MI5, all as nice as a Paris barber the lot of them. Maybe I am still at the top even to this very day. I don't know and I no longer care anyway. I certainly continued to give them more headaches than anyone else. In any event, the list is superficial but what they do to you when you reach the top is not. This I know from experience.
Richard Baker's brother was said to have grassed him in, and I thought the retard of a brother I have is torment with all the injustice he imposed upon me!
I only have a world ranking to rise from this position, but what little contacts I had within American Intelligence I never used to check the pecking order. Alternatively, someone down in England was offering to hack the FBI. This I found more interesting, but my objections to him doing so centered around concerns for his safety; it would have to be done in such a manner I were to take the full blame for it - British and American

Intelligence (and Israeli) having such a close working relationship where I am condemned by them anyway. Failing that, we would have to go to a hostile country like Iraq, Afghanistan or France to go hacking. They would have stringent security measures in place so he would only get low-grade intelligence. It is now the type of act I consider doing for no other reason than just for the hell of it.

1997 was the year two soldiers approached my home, which was nothing to be over alarmed at. Only, this pair were the most professional soldiers I ever seen. Both were tall powerful and athletic, dressed all in black with a backpack that had a pipe protruding straight up from the left shoulder - a gun barrel. As soon as I sighted them I was totally convinced these Men in Black were not average squaddies but were in fact SAS, where I knew from the circumstances I was their intended target. I was fortunate to survive this and afterwards given a tee-shirt from a former SAS member as a badge of respect. Not only did I survive the attack, I went out and crept up behind them to slit their throats knowing I would only get one of them before the other one finished me off. When I die I am not going to be lonely when I go to hell, somebody is going with me – an adversary will do nicely!

What was I really doing that night? Maybe I had read too many comics or watched too many action films where all great outlaws die in gun-battles, and decided; that's the one for me. The plan all went wrong as it unfolded where afterwards I was forced to run. Next time it would be different. I always run once, after that who knows what I will do?! In hindsight, it was definitely the right thing to do because they never made such a concerted effort to dispose of me again for a long time after. Once you have proven yourself more than a match for the best they have, what else is there? SAS members are regarded as being the best soldiers in the world. Not only that, I was now recalling the deed implying British Government involvement in the mass murder of unarmed civilians where many innocent people in the west of Scotland were already dead in similar circumstances! If I was found dead after this it would help verify what I, and many others, were claiming - those yet to be silenced?! One day the veneer will crack to reveal the truth, where my death could be the final incident in such a scenario!

This incident was followed with the suspected targeting of me for the murder of Jacqueline Gallacher. She was the fifth of five young women murdered from Glasgow's red light district where the basic facts about this murder went as follows: the city center business district of Blytheswood Square was originally Glasgow's center of prostitution (used for this purpose after business hours), but it got moved downhill from there to the Anderston district. Only an authority could be behind such a move, but, which one? In this new area, there are many government, national security and defense buildings with some of the most advanced security cameras available, but no positive sightings of any suspects has been made public from the footage in these cameras, although falsified pictures have been?! Likewise, such places are under twenty-four hour protection but no security guard ever presented any credible eye witness account for any of these murders. Glasgow city center has an extensive CCTV network covering this area; again no positive pictures were ever produced. You simply can't spit on the pavement here without being watched yet a mass murder of young women can take place unhindered! All the victims were murdered on Sunday nights/Monday mornings with similarities such as clothing being removed and physically assaulted prior to death, but the police refused to accept there was a serial killer operating. Interestingly enough, it was a Sunday night when I had a visit from the Men in Black where the shenanigans went on into the Monday morning, when at the time I was being set up as a wrongful suspect for this killing spree! Four out of the five died by strangulation with the other victim being drowned in the River Clyde. Over the spring and summer of 1995 the River Clyde had a weekly death toll, until a young woman escaped from a man trying to throw her into the water and then these killings suddenly and suspiciously ceased. Up until then them drowned in the Clyde had causes of death passed off either as suicide or accidental. The only notable death in the River Clyde after this episode was that of a five-year-old boy in 1998, whose father was wrongly convicted of murder then released from prison ten years previous. Against all perceived logic, nobody had been convicted for any of these strangulations or drownings. Further, the greatest death toll was of drug addicts at over a hundred a year from a relatively small population.

A *BBC Crimewatch* appeal had previously been made about the murder of Jackie Gallacher asking for evidence and witnesses concerning a black *BMW* car. The main suspect with the *BMW* was later found dead. At this, police made a press release saying they were no longer seeking anyone in connection with Jackie Gallacher's murder attempting to imply this innocent man was responsible. A second *BBC Crimewatch* appeal was shown on television after all this transpired without any mention of the *BMW* car, now that that targeted individual with such a vehicle was no longer with us. Instead, they focused the inquiry on a small red van with white writing and company logo. The description given of the wanted suspect, who was originally inconsistent with my features, now matched my description and details about the mode of transport corresponded with a brother's van. I did not have my own transport and often drove this van at the relevant time.

On the late Saturday morning, three days <u>before</u> the second *Crimewatch* appeal I was alone in the house when a burgundy *Land Rover* jeep with undercover personnel appeared outside, maneuvered into an awkward position then blasted the horn. Was it not for me viewing the situation from an upstairs window I would never have noticed a cameraman hidden in the backseat foot-well waiting to take a discreet photograph of me if I emerged from the front door to see what the commotion was? This helped dispel the notion any other family member was being targeted. Then on the following Saturday, four days after the *Crimewatch* appeal, all six bottles of milk on the doorstep had been tampered with. These bottles were found to have a virus syringed into them – a common dirty trick used by security forces in Northern Ireland in the nineteen-eighties on suspected terrorists before their arrest to weaken their resolve under interrogation. After leaving three samples of this milk with Strathclyde Police and waiting unsurprisingly nineteen days not to hear a reply, I departed a worried man for the safety of the European continent.

All this was complemented with the release of a pervert who was caught on the window-ledge of a victim but was freed to attack even more women. The photo-fit produced in an attempt to *catch* him afterwards bore no likeness to the assailant but a striking resemblance to me! Such a fabrication was presented in conjunction with the policeman leading the sham investigation sharing my name, which was greatly promoted in the press. This is a technique to have an altered perception of myself in the public eye by way of association. What is described here is a highly specialized trick playing with people's memories in a subliminal manner to alter the perception they have of someone prior to meeting them. Included in the many serious crimes listed here is attempted jury rigging by means of publicizing this dubious photo-fit together with the shared name, if I was to later stand trial for Jackie Gallacher's murder. Another less subtle way of achieving this is to have various newspaper stories all featuring the same crime, on the same page, and your name and photograph included on the same page. I was being subliminally connected to the sexual attack of women in facial likeness and by name before being targeted for the murder of a prostitute, which in the circumstances were two individual massive conspiracies interlinked. Furthermore, this did not appear genuine when I was being targeted in advance of the television appeal.

Up until then various attempts were made to convict people for these murders. Such suspects (innocents) had a nasty habit of being found dead afterwards. I was one of the few who was still alive but already had a confrontation with the Men in Black! Few people ever survive that.

On leaving all this behind, life was beautiful sleeping rough in the gutters of Portugal but the Great British authorities couldn't just let it be. Once I had come under surveillance of a cameraman there I sat up in the mountains around Braga to ponder what to do next. Strange how you remember incidents from the past relating to your present situation, such as listening to two of life's more entertaining characters saying how they were running out of countries to live in – a statement that never made too much sense upon hearing, though it did now. I couldn't outrun the authorities, so therefore in my crazy manner I would have to bite the bullet and turn around and face them. It is something about my nature I always run once, no matter how pathetic or serious the situation is, but after that…

Here was I, the very one to have known as a Scot growing up in an oppressed country under a foreign dictatorship demonstrations were pointless, democracy was dead, the media behaved like a propaganda service churning out State sponsored bile to misinform the masses, Scots Law had long been reduced to nothing more than a ridiculous piece of hypocrisy that only existed for the benefit of them of the right political persuasion or influence and was now at the point where it wasn't capable of delivering justice, the police were never known to provide any kind of service to resemble their supposed duty, and I was certain I couldn't change anything even if I wanted to, therefore knew never to take part in any demonstration or join any political party but was now contemplating fighting the corrupt system because I had no viable alternative. It is easy to look on as an outsider at the actions of political activists and terrorists and condemn them for what they did, but not all those people chose to fight, some were forced to. I was now undoubtedly forced to fight. The question I always ask to illustrate this is; what put the gun in Bobby Sands' hands? First you have to find the motive to understand the actions of others before you can criticize them. It is too easy to brand people without comprehending their situation.

One thing I had an abundance of was intelligence, coupled with the fact I was more than capable of most things, so in those Portuguese mountains I had plenty of time to consider all aspects of fighting. In addition to these attributes, where I was originally from was situated between two troubled cities, Glasgow and Belfast. Both have a religious divide with terrorist ramifications. There were always plenty of stories circulating from every side detailing terrorist and counter-terrorist campaigns and operations. The most successful terrorist group then was the Provisional IRA, so for this reason they would form a basis for my case study. It was only later did I discover I was not the first to sit down and analyze them in this manner, for some of the Loyalist terror groups had been so impressed by the success of their greatest enemy they tried to copy their tactics. Maybe the two sides were not poles apart after all! My study went deeper than what those Loyalists were looking at; all they wanted to do was ape the best military tactics and structuring of the Provisionals. I, in difference to them, wanted to consider the full picture. A case study it was…

Historically, Michael Collins led his group of IRA volunteers into Dublin from outlying areas only to be told by the city folk to 'go home', but in less polite language! From the 1916 Easter Uprising within six years they achieved the Free State that later became the Republic of Ireland. Timing had been helpful because the British Army were fighting the First World War and didn't want a second front opening up on what they regarded home soil. At the time of national recognition, wealth of Ireland and greater Protestant population were both centered on the Province of Ulster, so Britain retained what was referred to as the Six Counties splitting Ireland in two. Creating a country in this manner was a historic anomaly; for the Province of Ulster was traditionally larger than those Six Counties and was never previously recognized with an independent national identity. Some would dispute this with historic claims but their evidence is at best sketchy. In the remaining years of the nineteen-sixties a new faction was formed breaking away from the IRA; they were the Provisional IRA. Remnants of Michael Collins' IRA then became known as the Official IRA with a small splinter group also rising in a direct line from them called the INLA - Irish National Liberation Army. They were small and volatile with less political aspirations attached compared to other groupings. So when the Provisional IRA took up arms over forty years ago, they were also ridiculed like predecessors when the initials were mocked for supposedly meaning: I Ran Away. Had tormentors any inclination as to what was to materialize from this humiliating start they would never have been so condescending. The Provisional IRA grew from humble beginnings to allegedly become the most professional terrorist army in the world. They are regarded as being entirely Roman Catholic, although in its secret conception it is hinted Protestant Irishmen were also members or closely associated. Michael Collins rejected this religious divide when he led his Republican Army, where it is open to question whether the British Secret Service sought to eradicate any Protestants from the Provisionals, fittingly with their common tactic of divide and conquer. The green and orange (separated by white) in the Irish tricolor flag are there to represent the Catholic and Protestant communities respectively. Without such integration, Republicans could never win in a democratic process held solely in Northern Ireland because a slight majority of the population are Protestant. It became them and us, Catholic against Protestant, British fighting Irish, the same situation that marred Irish politics for centuries. With every bullet fired and every bomb exploded the two communities separated even further with mistrust and hatred rife.

The two biggest events to change attitudes and the course of events in recent times in the Province of Ulster were Bloody Sunday and the suicide of IRA hunger striker Bobby Sands. Bombs and bullets may have been instrumental in bringing these incidents about, where they remain the actual turning points. Bloody Sunday was when the British Army shot dead thirteen unarmed protesters in Derry/Londonderry in 1972 at a civil rights march where neither the Provisional IRA nor Official IRA retaliated in any manner (INLA being smaller and not always present in a military capacity). Those injured and killed at the demonstration were from both communities.

Bobby Sands was the first hunger striker to die in the Maze Prison in 1981. He died highlighting the Irish Nationalist struggle. The Provisional IRA benefited immensely by means of support and new recruits from both events. When Sands starved himself to death, afterwards there was the reflective joke, 'Margaret Thatcher; the (wo)man that built the Provisional IRA', such was the support garnished. Up until then the Provisionals were relatively small with a threat posed that was more or less containable until this happened. Afterwards their operations, success and audacity multiplied ten-fold. That standoff between Thatcher and Sands was the greatest single event in the Province of Ulster to change the course of modern history. Once again, it was neither a bomb nor a bullet from any terrorist/freedom fighter to altered things so dramatically...

Nineteen-eighties became the heyday of the Provisionals, for they even managed to hit their number one target, the detested

Mrs. Thatcher, at the Conservative Party Conference in a hotel in Brighton. Patrick Magee was the man responsible. He previously hid a bomb in one of the toilets waiting for the political gathering to take place to have it detonated when the politicians arrived, and became known afterwards as the Brighton Bomber. The other bombings in London of the Baltic Exchange and Canary Wharf were the three explosions to change attitudes on mainland British soil. Up until then it was regarded as a conflict being fought in another part of the world to most mainland British people, then all of a sudden it was on their doorstep. All three explosions happened in England; could the Provisionals not learn from this? Take the fight to the enemy, that sort of thing. Their success, and affront of attacking Thatcher with the Conservative cabinet, would only lead to more draconian methods in an effort to cripple them from the middle eighties onwards. This, and the greater introduction of technology into a rapidly changing world, would lead to a diplomatic settlement in the near future. A small band of rebels opposed the deal settled on the day in 1998 that gave it its name, the 'Good Friday Agreement', to form the Real IRA and also Continuity IRA, but in general most members refrained from violence.

All along the British Government had been in secret negotiations to try to end the conflict, but for public consumption the view broadcast was they, 'Don't negotiate with terrorists'.

Margaret Thatcher and British Royal Family, as a wholly Protestant and British institution (only in recent times are Roman Catholics allowed to marry into the Royal Family though not to become monarch), were their two greatest targets where the uncle of Prince Charles, Lord Mountbatten, was murdered in 1979 before the campaign of violence intensified in the next decade. He had lived at Mullaghmore, one of Ireland's more beautiful seaside locations on the Atlantic coast. I liked to walk along that beach even with knowledge of what had happened out in the sea there, and in doing so could unintentionally understand the beauty and tragedy of recent Irish history. A sentiment probably shared by many Irish when they accept how their nation was formed and who they once opposed.

Attitudes slowly changed towards the Provisional IRA in the Republic of Ireland as young men and women grew up on that side of the border without the troubles of the past, which has become memories of grandparents and great-grandparents. Plus, wealth in the Republic was rising fast with people there more concerned about stocks and shares than past events. Ireland, which was partitioned in the nineteen-twenties, now had a new phenomenon to contend with, North/South hatred to go along with prevailing national and religious bigotry. Many in the South (and particularly in the North) may well hate the British Army, but realized a dead British soldier still had his friends and family, dreams and fears, where his loss was just the same to that of a neighbor or friend. No longer, in their name, did they want any more killing.

My case study concluded the Provisional IRA were annexed by three fundamental faults: One, in a democratic process they needed some of the Protestant/Unionist population of Northern Ireland to vote in their favor (a united Ireland) but ever present violence created ever widening divisions where no member of the other community was going to support the opposition: Two, support had risen in the nineteen-eighties when the world was changing into the electronic age making their military strategy and operations outdated (it did give rise to more sophisticated bomb making): And three; the greater population of Ireland, who now ironically consider themselves in favor of Collins and his IRA group, were now rejecting violence completely therefore many no longer laid claim to the other Six Counties fearing continuing violence would flow into their neighborhood should they unite. Furthermore, in the South religious bigotry is less profound, where again the greater Irish population didn't want this syndrome to escalate.

As part of the deal struck in the Good Friday Agreement, the Republic of Ireland denounced its territorial claim to the Province of Ulster for the first time in the country's short history. This was agreed to appease Unionist suspicions' a secret deal had been brokered. *Sinn Fein* now recognizes the inherent problems associated with the Provisionals' campaign and have taken steps to adjust to a new political climate of peace. Slowly and awkwardly Unionists were forced to change stance.

The Loyalist Ulster Defense Association (UDA) were said to have studied the Provisional IRA and developed cells similar to rivals, which meant upon arrest no single person could betray the entire organization. Only those inside the Loyalist terror groups can answer what military operations they copied. So here was I looking at the whole picture realizing how futile firepower had become, and what was more certain I couldn't shoot my way out of the position I found myself in but having said that, I had very little to lose, whereas the dictatorship oppressing the Scottish nation had it all to lose. Further, I doubted if I would ever get to load the first gun before I would be disposed of such were the circumstances. Otherwise, it was time to fight, to fight a different kind of war.

To have noted the Provisionals were fighting a forlorn conflict with the wrong methods and strategy I needed to find an alternative role model to copy that was successful in recent times; the answer came in the guise of the Cold War. Sidelining of the Provisionals could be compared to the Mafia, where they have become something of a relic from the past with antiquated rules and dress sense running protection rackets instead of indulging in more sophisticated crimes such as electronic fraud where the real money is. FBI goons continue to chase them (some would argue needlessly) in a game of cops and robbers.

So what really won the Cold War? Truth is those spies with satellites were just playing at James Bond and had little impact on the situation. So what were the deciding factors? It was all a lot more subtle than that, it was a cultural change, a change in attitudes, whereby demonstrating to those behind the Iron Curtain there was a better alternative, a new way of life, a dream on offer if they rejected communism. In contrast to all the nuclear arsenals both sides stockpiled, it was simple things like literature, religion and freedom of expression that made the difference! What military strategist could have foreseen this? Once political discontent got a foothold in the shipyards of Poland soon people in other countries were about to follow, where with it the fall of communism was like a domino effect from when the Berlin Wall fell onwards.

Many behind the former Iron Curtain felt betrayed once Western practices were adopted, but it was the promise that sold the philosophy...

Was I really going to fight the British Government with the pen? I never believed the pen to be mightier than the sword. It was an optimistic statement contrived by some frustrated author long forgotten. Would I turn to religion? Religion (Christianity in particular) that was failing rapidly in modern Western society, and I, for one, had little faith – although in the future I did become Muslim?! How could I get freedom of expression when the facts were always being habitually stifled by Government means? What I did believe was the truth would sicken ordinary folk and change attitudes, thereby I had to expose it by whatever means possible, even if this meant by the proverbial pen. Such exposure that should be guaranteed in a democracy is hard to come by in a crippled situation. Alternatively, there were other ways of confronting the evil regime before me in a practice of hearts and minds...

On return from Portugal fully focused upon what was required, but, this was marred with the next attack on me by a second police force. Once again they were to use the *BBC Crimewatch* program *imaginatively* when a second reconstruction was shown of the double murder of Lin and Megan Russell. Both mother and young daughter were bludgeoned to death with a hammer, or by some other blunt instrument, where the elder daughter, Josie, present survived. She went on to recover remarkably from the fractured skull and brain damage received. The second reconstruction of this crime had all my details included, even going so far as having the photo-fit person with a buckled stance shown outside his car, yet bizarrely the suspect was never seen standing to depict such a stance?! However, it corresponded with me having a shattered ankle where at times I found it was impossible to hold an upright posture. The facial photo-fit image held a photographic likeness to me. The original suspect never shared any features in common and was depicted with distinctive broad shoulders that also vanished in the second appeal. But, it was the car that proved most contentious, where in the first reconstruction, shown a year previous, it had been a brown *Ford Escort*. Now it miraculously changed color into a red *Escort* as it drove down the road! The last car I owned was, fittingly, for this as a fit-up, a red *Ford Escort*. For a second time it was obvious I had been targeted in advance of the reconstruction being shown. On that night, the broadcast was live with television presenter Jill Dando where she picked up on the many ludicrous discrepancies shown and proceeded to ask the policeman in the studio about such ridiculous antics. One and three-quarter years later she was found murdered on her own doorstep with a single bullet to the head. She died a heroine for highlighting some of the many anomalies in this case. She also died refusing to be manipulated by those behind the scenes, thereby exposing the truth about a grotesque crime with a certain amount of corruption attached to the investigation procedures. My founding principle of changing attitudes in this manner, were exemplified by her actions.

My campaign got off to a bad start, whereon viewing this program I knew people would recognize me from it as a child killer. They did, and I now had the stigma of being a pedophile locally due to what they'd done. It was the most corrupt vile and evil thing I ever experienced. In the middle of summer, there was I sitting in the back of the shed with the lights out unable to face the world anymore where for two weeks sickness was running down the front of my shirt at the mere thought of such a stigma. It couldn't get much worst. I planned on reinventing terrorism to fight the evils of the British Government, but it would be a long time before I recuperated from this incident. Their depth of depravity is demonstrated in this episode, likewise I could only do well by comparison when up against them in support of child killers...

In Scotland, there had been small terrorist outbreaks in the past but by the year 1997 there was no longer any such groups to align with. Willie McCrae was a Glasgow lawyer dubbed the Godfather of Scottish terrorism until he was found dead on a remote mountainside in the Scottish Highlands in 1980. He too had been shot in the head. What he was credited with was forming the Willie McCrae Commandos, or from the initials, the WMC. A campaign centered on burning holiday homes belonging to English people in Scotland, such a practice was later repeated in Wales. Plus, an attempt to kidnap Princess Anne, which sounded more like a fantasy dreamt up by some goon in London to distract from matters?! After this a second terrorist group emerged called the SNLA; Scottish National Liberation Army. They were small whose activities ended in the middle nineteen-nineties upon arrests and with others going into exile. A limited bombing campaign attacking soft targets like power lines was as far as they aspired too. Both groups used conventional methods to take the fight to the enemy, which was not what I was looking for having learned from surveying Ireland where the bomb and bullet were no longer a successful means of fighting unless targets were strategically chosen offering little offense to the overall population. Another example of this being limited in scope was when the Brighton Bomber struck. He was hunted down like a dog afterwards (to be captured in Glasgow of all places), whereas what I was about to do never held the same repercussions but could remove the most senior of people from British society and reveal how bad it really was for the population of Scotland. It was time to fight but with bloodless tactics. What I started with was a strategy superbly masterminded given a little inside information... With which, what could be achieved would soon surpass all expectations alleging to have removed politicians and senior police officers alike, where the number of whom (and others) quickly ran into double figures. Maybe one day, whatever Irish terrorists still active will reverse the trend to learn a little something from me! From 1997 onwards, all combined success of all terrorists and groups operating within the British Isles could not match my run of victories! I was, quite simply, in an unique category.

In keeping with these philosophies, both sides of the sectarian divide within the Province of Ulster already have a cultural aspect to their campaigns with many splendid murals painted on walls within respective communities, plus folk songs in glorification. They both adopted the same piece of the historic Scottish document, the Declaration of Arbroath, which was signed back in 1320, with the uncompromising nationalistic passage: -

For, as long as but a hundred of us remain alive, never will we on any condition be brought to English rule. It is in truth not for glory, nor riches, nor honors that we are fighting, but for freedom – for that alone, which no honest man surrenders but with his life.

The word *English* substituted by *British, Irish* or *Papist* rule depending on the author writing with whatever outlook – Irish, British or Protestant respectively. Strange how two sides can be so bitter towards each other yet share so much, usually from a Scottish source – Declaration of Arbroath, Highland bagpipes, Scots language, customs, traditions, etc. The difference being Irish Nationalists share most in common with West Highland culture whereas Ulster Unionists adopted practices of Lowland Scots of whom they claim descent.

And; why was I in this position? Why was I, as the most reluctant and unlikely political activist (dissident or terrorist), now about to confront the evil of British rule? Why did I earn a reputation that didn't correspond with my personality? Metaphorically; what put the gun in my hands? Some local trouble escalated out of hand of which I had little involvement, but it brought me to police attention. No longer could I sandbag my way through life. No longer could I be an anonymous face in a crowd who never wanted to oppose anything, let alone the tyranny subjected to. No longer could I pretend it was never happening or it didn't affect me, just like I and so many others did in the past. My middle brother was inclined to go into town and cause trouble then run away every time. I had no objections to him doing this if he would for once sort out the problems created, unfortunately for me this was never going to happen. He was too dense to realize what he was doing and had basically never grown up. One day he did have to walk like a man, with me no longer there where I can never return to live in Scotland such are my circumstances, and when that day came he found it a very different world. The thing is people like this never comprehend what they are doing, or in his case likely too. They just leave a trail of chaos behind them for others to deal with. In this scenario it was an escalating nightmare. I was always the unfortunate one left to clean up all the shit he created.

This is an over simplified version of events, where in basic terms the problems I faced were by and large manufactured by the authorities for whatever reason. Included in this were means by which they could attempt to cover up their crimes. Where on viewing the community as individuals it was easy for them to victimize innocent people one-by-one. A situation so vile and intricate that it is difficult to comprehend, equally so, it is difficult to put a concerted effort together to confront. As individuals they will find ways of compromising each and every one of them. Those responsible must have laughed when they first selected me to be targeted; a small quiet person who never really came to their attention. Someone that lived half-way up a mountain with little interest in crime or politics, and, as far as they were concerned, I was never going to know shit from toffee. On the surface I must have looked like the easiest victim they could pick upon. How wrong they were. Evil as they are, but when the casualties started multiplying on their side, including deaths of their personnel, I wonder if they are still laughing now – probably not.

'...for the warriors whose strength is not to fight.'

3. STRATEGY.

'I liked Bill, he was probably below average intelligence with no outstanding features, but in his favor, he was a storyteller. Both he and a friend would find a posh restaurant in the West End of Glasgow and then start a conversation along the following lines, "Have you got the shotguns, I've got the ski-masks; we hit that bank across the road at 4 O' clock."
Bill's friend would agree in a stern voice and serious look to continue the conversation along the same track. The two of them would look out of place dressed in black leather bikers' jackets, jeans and working boots surrounded by pretentious people wearing fur coats and shiny shoes. Such people had never lived for one moment in their entire lives, nor likely to, therefore never know, upon overhearing this conversation, Bill and his companion were never going to rob anything.'

September the Eleventh will always be remembered for those two airplanes crashing into the World Trade Center Twin Towers in New York. Call it being skeptical, cynicism or whatever, but I remain one of the few that fail to remember this date for that reason, but for another momentous event. Surprising as it sounds, I always think of the Scottish Battle of Stirling Brig when Scottish patriot William Wallace defeated the English army there on the same day in the year 1297. This was also the day in 1997 pervert Grant McCaskill was sentenced to ten years imprisonment where this incident features and has a personal bearing here.

The historic character of William Wallace became universally known when Mel Gibson produced the Hollywood film *'Braveheart'*. To me this was where terrorism began. Wallace only ever held one battle-plan when fighting rivals - that being, never to fight a battle! The film did hint at this but never portrayed it properly. Back in those days Scots picked off stragglers from the invading army and scouts that preceded it into the country. They burnt their own crops and slaughtered their animals to starve the English out of the country. Ambushes and small guerrilla attacks undermined morale where with it English occupation. My old grandfather, William Watson, told stories about this period in Scottish history then went on to claim, 'The Watsons were the right-hand men to William Wallace'. Tales of a grandfather for you, told in front of an open fire just like it should be. It took me years to realize; didn't every lowland Scottish clan claim to be the right-hand men to William Wallace?! Watsons were not even Scots for they originated from County Antrim Ireland. He also claimed the Watsons were a family of Jews; I am still trying to fathom this out because we have been Christians for as far back as I know. Maybe I never will, or maybe that is the point, that I never will, and now *Auld Wullie* (and his eldest daughter, my mother) is gone there is little hope of discovering the truth. For all this, I just loved those stories about Wallace fighting the English with their severed heads rolling down the mountain-sides. We were Scots and proud of it; I later read graffiti in the local pub toilet saying words to this effect; *'SNLA, we are Scots'*.

No self-respecting activist is complete without a history lesson. Where I had had mine from my father who constantly read Scottish history and grandfather with his tales about Wallace and the rural county of Ayrshire. His stories were all much localized. The Irish are great at preserving their history, but it is not just them that fought for the 'cause' that can constantly remind you of eight hundred years of English come British brutality. Scotland, in the same vein, can claim a thousand years of English brutality but few Scots ever broach the subject for fear of offending their southern neighbors. What Scottish history I read or knew of never led me to favoring patriots like William Wallace, Robert De Bruce, King James IV, Bonnie Dundee (Graham of Claverhouse), Rob Roy McGregor, Flora McDonald or Bonnie Prince Charlie (Charles Edward Stewart). No; I found King Billy Marshall one of life's more entertaining characters. He was king of the Galloway tinkers and often fought with the British Army when as a young man in the regiment of the Grey Scots, including at the Battle of Boyne (1690) in Ireland. Grey Scots were a rough bunch made up from the dregs of society with Marshall being one of their more notorious characters. He lived to be a hundred-and-twenty, had nineteen wives and over a hundred children and was known to participate in every crime imaginable yet retain a sense of fair-play. He is one of those people they exclude from the history books in case future generations realize there is an alternative to a dull boring life such is the sanitized world we live in. However, his legend prevails by word of mouth plus his mark is still prevalent with descendants bearing a black spoon birthmark on the back of their hands...

As for strategy, in the context relating to what I was planning to achieve, I looked at the banking industry for guidance! I went through life with a different outlook and this is just another example of an alternative thought process. At this you will automatically think of money laundering, but that was not where my education came from. That is nothing other than a straight forward means of hiding money from criminal enterprises. Otherwise, if you have been more alert you will think of electronic fraud, again, this is not what I'm talking about. This will be found unbelievable, but banking was the primary source of all my exploits. Want a lesson in terrorism, are you considering taking on a Western government, then go and ask your local bank manager for guidance?! Somehow it doesn't sound right especially so when you view him as the most boring person on the planet. However, in recent times it became obvious to the general public how ruthless and corrupt this industry really is, so in hindsight all I really got was advanced warning...

For a quick explanation of this principle, take a country like England for example; the banking industry is full of highly intelligent people but the basic product has never changed in two-thousand years when the Romans brought coins into the country. So what is this industry doing with all its brain power? Why do such intelligent people need to be employed in a company/industry with no realistic product advances in the future? Honesty could be a convenient answer unless you know a little more about the level of corruption this industry conceals. Takeovers and mergers come to mind, and the manner in which they are accomplished. It is not usually done in an upstanding way!

How is success achieved when you are the third segment of a trio looking to triumph over two more powerful rivals? This is not done by you going in opposition with either, but by giving your backing to the weaker of the two so to instill enough confidence in them to confront the greater rival then capitalize at the outset once they weaken each other. Has the United States not being doing this in most major conflicts fought in the world until recent times where they have now became the aggressor? History recalls the United States entering the Second World War in Europe near the conclusion, whereon backing the winning side amidst allegations they were going to side with Germany. They carried off the spoils of war in the aftermath, especially so when *NASA* was founded with many German scientists brought over in *Operation Paperclip.*

Alternatively, how does a bank reward them that are favored without amassing any suspicion out with the parties involved? The answer is by sponsoring their football team for example. It is all done in such a subtle manner no one would realize it has happened. Bank's logo is a common fixture on many different places so when it appears on a favored subject, whose to tell why this is?

I learnt all my tactics from the banking industry at a time when I no longer had a bank account just to complete the paradox! This was because I was even forced to close my personal account under suspicious circumstances.

From here, I now possessed nationalistic historic grievances, present day oppression to oppose, and personal injustice all intertwined with the bank managers' tactics. It was time to put them into practice with the instincts of a terrorist and methods used in the Cold War. As for targets, they would present themselves once matters progressed/digressed. You have to understand Scottish society a little better to realize how difficult it is to confront the system there. Newspapers and television companies are either English based or owned expressly planted with those from the British Establishment and have little intention in exposing Scottish discrimination within Scotland. Such an opinion voiced would help the Nationalist movement, therefore it simply doesn't happen. When the SNP finally came to power their leader once stated he'd never been interviewed by the major broadsheet newspaper *The* Scotsman – more on that later. The law is an even more curious beast, never offending or opposing English tyranny yet it has a constant stream of English people who win cases of discrimination, likewise there was a run of police officers claiming compensation for minor incidents when just doing their supposed duties. Scottish police forces swear allegiance to the Queen and not to the people they are meant to provide a service for. Political parties in opposition to a unionist viewpoint are under Secret Service surveillance offering little prospect of opposing anything thereby killing off democracy in the process (Scotland is a sovereign nation in her own right therefore the Secret Service cannot justify this action inside a democratic framework). On official figures, Scots are twice as likely to be under Secret Service surveillance compared with English neighbors. You have to ask why? Especially so with a lower crime rate and a greater percentage of law abiding citizens in Scotland?! In the face of all this, Scots are quite literally second class citizens in their own country, scandalous as it is. There simply is nowhere to turn to if you find yourself on the wrong side of the British Establishment. It is always assumed or portrayed (by the media behaving like a propaganda service) you are the cause of the issue. How can you get your message out in these circumstances? More accurately, how can you get the truth out in such corrupt circumstances?

In Northern Ireland Republicans formed their own political parties and printed newspapers to oppose British rule. In doing so, this is an expensive complicated and time consuming method of furthering objectives, but it always was the long war for them involved. Such is the circumstances there, people readily accept 'just another murder' or 'political gesture' where momentous actions no longer have the same impact on public opinion in the manner they would have elsewhere in the Western world. People become war weary after too many years of strife.

In my case when the second reconstruction was shown on *Crimewatch* about Lin and Megan Russell I was left in such a state I was virtually paralyzed, from which I would recuperate to launch a first major attack four months later.

When I deposited three bottles of milk with the police I never slept that night but contemplated the scenario and came to the daunting conclusion this life expectancy was not great given the context. Days later I bolted into the night only to be stopped the next afternoon on what was now an illegal motorcycle, due to a change in the law, and given a minor motoring charge. This violation was brought to court. The first good opportunity to oppose the tormentors presented itself when a trial materialized from this incident. Here was I with no faith whatsoever in Scots Law about to face a minor motoring offense that would give a £50 fine regardless of protestations, which was ideal to use as a platform to air some grievances. It was time to abuse what I perceived a corrupt system to my advantage. On the morning of the court-case I left early to take a detour on going to the court-house to telephone various newspapers saying a story was about to break in Greenock District Court that day concerning Glasgow's murdered prostitutes. Hopefully this would intrigue journalists, give them the scent, to attract them to the scene. My exploits were to be aired under oath thereby giving no legal implications to the press if they chose to print the story. At the time I felt short-changed when only one freelance journalist and two others from the Glasgow based *Evening Times* appeared. My woes multiplied soon after I started delivering my defense with the case being adjourned for legal discussion in the barrister's backroom chambers. When the judge reappeared he insisted testimony could only be given in mitigation. Although circumstances weren't favorable, the story featured two days later in the Glasgow based *Evening Times* newspaper, where with two corresponding photographs it read: -

I'M BEING FRAMED

MAN MAKES BIZARRE MURDER CLAIMS IN COURTROOM

A man has stunned a Scottish court by claiming police are out to frame him for the murder of Glasgow prostitute Jackie Gallacher. His claims form a tangled web that pulls together murder, rape, attempted murder and international intrigue.
Robert Rae says he lives "in fear for his life."
He made a complex string of allegations to back his claim, including his alleged portrayal by the police as a sex fiend behind the attacks on 20 women and the killing of six ... including vice girl Jackie Gallacher. He admits driving a red Renault van in the Glasgow area ... cops have linked the driver of such a van to the unsolved Gallacher probe.
PHOTOFIT
The girl was found wrapped in a carpet in a lay-by near Bowling. Rae also claims the police photo-fit issued prior to the arrest and conviction of Grant McCaskill – who got life earlier this year for stalking Glasgow women after his girlfriend shopped him – bears a resemblance to himself.
Jackie (26) was brutally slain and her body dumped in a lay-by on the Glasgow-Dumbarton road last June. Now Rae has put himself firmly in the spotlight. Yesterday, he amazed officials at Inverclyde District Court where he was on trial for a minor motoring offence. He declared: "I am being framed for the murder of prostitute Jackie Gallacher."

Rae (29) was charged with driving his 125cc motorcycle without a Basic Training Certificate. When magistrate Ronald McEwan asked what Rae's defense was, the unemployed cabinet-maker stormed: "I fled my home at 4.20am in fear of my life and to prevent a major scandal breaking. The scandal involves the attacking of about 20 women, six of whom were murdered. The police are actively framing me for the murder of Jackie Gallacher."

SHOOTING
He claims that a police photo-fit released during the West End manhunt identified him. He claims that he frequently used his brother's red Renault van – similar to one being sought in connection with the murder – to drive into Glasgow. He also claims that he is an eyewitness to a gangland shooting in Beith and this makes him the subject of police interest.

The two traffic cops who flagged him down in Greenock – Constables Patrick Martin and David Ryan – sat stunned in court. The magistrate found Rae guilty and fined him £50. Afterwards, Rae said he was "doing a runner" – possibly back to Portugal or France, where he says he slipped through an Interpol net earlier this year. A leading detective working on the Jackie Gallacher murder team said: "I can categorically deny that Strathclyde Police frame anybody. This is a live inquiry and it would be wrong to identify people we have, or have not, interviewed."

This was my first step in challenging the tyranny faced - I would later learn in history Adolph Hitler did a similar ploy?! Tactics were good leaving it all to the last minute then springing a surprise on everyone, especially the security forces giving them no time to react. The truth is it shouldn't be this way, as I'd previously approached newspapers holding samples of milk I claimed were contaminated with a virus but after discussions from 'upstairs' they declined to independently analysis it, presumably because of the risk of exposing involvement of Government agencies. Then they like to call this a democracy, where again, maybe my description of a foreign dictatorship is more accurate. Was that not a massive story where they poison innocent people then attempt to frame them for murder? This was happening in cases where the actual suspects were found dead afterwards, and I had already been visited by the Men in Black! Or what about all the women who were needlessly attacked by the pervert they released in an attempt to rig any future jury against me?! How much more serious or scandalous can it become before the so-called free press act to forewarn and protect the public against this ridiculously evil regime? Why do they continue to ignore or conceal the obvious with the population suffering so much? Yet, they continually pump out propaganda telling the people about what a wonderful deal they are getting. Certain journalists will be left questioning their ethics, because they know the truth but have conspired in promoting this treachery. The law also has assisted greatly in the scenario by never trying them involved but allows innocent people to be wrongly tried (and found guilty on occasions!) where them within the corrupt legal profession also know what is happening.

A few weeks later I read in another newspaper a woman had done a similar stunt when she had no tax disc on a car and had also used her court-case to expose her persecution. I laughed, wondering if she'd copied my tactics then continued to question the position she had found herself in. Did she also find out the so called free Press were no longer so in Scotland? Desperate for exposure to halt her persecution, did she have to find an alternative way of accomplishing this? I would not be surprised.

In regards to actual success or failure of my exposure, on return to the workshop I attended in Cumnock I found a disgruntled supervisor saying his council employment had been terminated immediately after this exploit. I had been suspicious about his actions previously, therefore never told him what I was about to do because SNLA terrorists that came into this workshop alleged at the time of their arrest this supervisor was informing on them. Now here, most certainly by my actions, he was suddenly removed.

When you consider the two different methods of fighting the system, what hope did those terrorists have of dealing with him? A bullet in the head, perhaps? Their men were either imprisoned or on the run at this point without anyone left capable of confronting him. Where of them, the one who could be considered to have the most potential for such an act was their leader, but he lived in exile never returning home.

This method of mass exposure was about the only one open to me at the time, but in doing so the furor it caused was astounding. My half-witted brother was in his element afterwards because it gave him a platform to spout some of the nonsense that filled his head when traveling around the countryside telling people I had went insane; up to this point most believed the reverse to be true. It was incidents like him traveling two hundred miles from home to tell an uncle that really made his motives questionable, but this relative questioned why he was going to such extremes (four hundred miles) to damage my reputation thereby putting the onus back on him, or a mate who had a similar complaint. Upon challenging this friend on the subject I was left somewhat bewildered saying, "But, he doesn't even talk to you."

He agreed to also find it strange how this foolish brother was behaving. What was happening here? I always alleged his girlfriend was an undercover agent where she was manipulating this stubborn character, which given his stupid ridiculous nature and the way he'd done me every injustice imaginable all his life, mostly unknown to him such is his stubbornness and stupidity, this was so easy to do.

Since the age of sixteen when I tried to out-run a police car on a moped, I'd been a regular visitor to the court on motoring offenses so no amount of nonsense spouted after could justify my actions that day other than what the truth was. To put it all in perspective, here was someone who once drove home from the local disco with three passengers that mysteriously vanished, beginning when Maureen in the passenger seat claimed, "Stuart's on the roof."

A mile or so later with me unable to squint into the backseat foot-well to find where he was hiding, she then announced, "Stuart and Morna are on the roof."

On hearing this I couldn't believe what she was saying until Stuart looked in, upside-down from the outside of the windscreen, at which I put the wipers and washers on to clean his face. I pleaded with Maureen not to do it, but she also went up to join them. With all three holding onto the roof-rack it wasn't the tires that were screeching as I circled the local round-about at speed trying to knock them off!

There was always going to be retribution by this tyrannical regime for what I did. The next incident after this joint court-case/newspaper arrangement was when I complained bed sheets were substituted on my bed. This is a known underhand practice when the authorities want a DNA sample. Then just days after, another Glasgow prostitute, Tracey Wilde, was again strangled on another Sunday night/Monday morning. I had every reason to believe my DNA was now planted at the murder scene. Can you imagine that; a newspaper story connecting me to six murdered women when the general population only really knew of five, with the possibility of my DNA planted on a sixth victim. The actual sixth victim in my article was Lin Russell, but others would not make the connection and with any forthcoming court case against me it would be concealed; no doubt?! At this point, I once again resigned myself to the fact it was all over. A strange state of affairs materialized from this when the first report was of a man in a blue *Ford Escort* witnessed leaving the victim's flat at 2AM. I was also at this time under surveillance by a man in a blue *Ford Escort* who matched the description of the wanted suspect.

The first television report on Tracey Wilde's murder showed what appeared to be Special Branch favored *BT* (British Telecom) vans at the crime scene, and, with a jubilant Police Chief Constable, John Orr, talking on another subject in the same news bulletin?! From this, you can surmise how bad the conditions are for the native people…

In other countries by having my story in print, albeit limited in incriminating substance and of a slightly confused nature, this would be sufficient to scare off the authorities or have the claims independently investigated, but not in Scotland where their only concern is to continue the killings and persecution.

Now it was back to the waiting game. I would pass five months before my next attack, sitting there sweating it out with every reason to believe my DNA was now at a murder scene that would result in my wrongful conviction. Although desperate to reveal who I believed to be responsible for this latest killing, I knew tactics and timing had to be perfect to secure the right kind of result. It would be a one shot affair so there could be no room for error. There is also the major problem of exposing who is involved if they are assisted or connected in any way to the British authorities. If you were to try and get a newspaper or a television company interested in Government, Secret Service or police corruption in Scotland you will find it nearly impossible and because of this the whole population suffers in what is in effect a police state where the authorities have a free reign to do as they please. They know this and abuse the situation accordingly only keeping a thin veneer of accountability. This is how it has been for longer than I care to remember, and what I viewed in youth as rule by a foreign dictatorship maybe has a lot of credence to it. Even once they are well and truly caught out their attitude is, 'We did it and so what; there is nothing you can do about it anyway'. As for the law, I can never recall it once challenging the British Government. I may be wrong on the subject or it was in the distant past, but no, I cannot give an example. This again, with them accused of so much is the definition of a dictatorship. Undeterred, I would find an alternative method of exposure where my next tactic was the 'Press release'.

First of all I went to indulge in a little graffiti, when I spelt the next victim's first name wrongly where the security forces would never suspect the message about to be produced actually belonged to me if I gave the correct spelling in it. Further, it was also important they knew this act of graffiti was mine, but only in a subtle manner so not to over emphasize my real intention. Onward I went to make up a photocopied message alleging who (Special Branch Officer Raymond Stevenson) I believe killed Tracey Wilde. This written allegation was made up with no forensic evidence connecting me to it then posted to various newspapers.

What I was trying to do here was pretend somebody disgruntled inside the security forces produced the message then sent it to the press. An anonymous surprise attack it would be once again.

The timing of such an action coincided with the release of details concerning a bungled investigation into a child murder. This argument between the Chief Constable of Grampian Police and Henry McLeish MP was blown up out of all proportions. The question to be answered here is; did the authorities use this bungled investigation, and the resulting report from it, as a means of persuading whoever leaked the information in my photocopy to cease their activities thinking the disclosures came from inside the Intelligence community? I can only state the facts which wholeheartedly support this view…

A tabloid newspaper had a front page exposé of the discrepancies included in the child murder case on the morning before posting the photocopied messages to the press. A day and a half later there was a commentary on both the radio and television stations about the leak of, 'confidential information' said to be, 'irresponsible of the person doing this' and, 'how damaging this type of thing was to the police'. A further announcement claimed what was now going to be released in connection with the bungled child murder would be, 'The most damning report on the police since the War'. The press were stated as already being in possession of all this damning information yet mysteriously had nothing to print on the subject, which was a massive contradiction to then be complemented by a telltale omission when it was announced it would be in the Sunday newspapers! This gave a puzzling three day delay for an unknown reason, unless they were buying time to make a fabrication to correspond with what they claimed?! When the Sunday newspapers appeared there was nothing to correspond with what was previously claimed (*The most damning report on the police since the war*) but only the original allegations repeated! The only thing that happened in the intervening period was the Chief Constable, Dr. Oliver, accusing Henry McLeish MP of breaking a verbal agreement and of him being the instigator behind a tabloid newspaper front page headline, '*I WILL SHAME YOU*', directed at the police chief. Again, this possessed no substance whatsoever, especially when McLeish started to lose the argument to then suspiciously disappear from the heated disagreement.

So I decided to complicate the matter, believing I was indeed the source of this (what was potentially a double-meaning) argument, by sending out more of my messages where by design they would arrive on the Monday morning to expect a response later that day. Donald Dewar, who at the time was the most senior politician in the country upon being Secretary for State of Scotland, appeared on television from inside the House of Commons (British Parliament) concerning the ongoing argument. When addressing the Chief Constable, un-characteristically he furiously told him to, "Pack your bags and go, now".

For two weeks this row rattled on where every tactic imaginable, including dirty tricks by the Government side, were used to remove the Chief Constable until he finally announced his retirement. When he did decide to depart after a backroom briefing(?!), surprisingly, Donald Dewar and Labour Party councilor Pat Chambers both acknowledged his achievements in their farewell speeches with Chambers having to apologize for remarks he previously made - he claimed the police chief was holding out for a larger financial settlement, which was not true, but it assisted in demonizing the Chief Constable. In the end this Chief Constable (one of eight in Scotland) publicly accused the most senior politician, Donald Dewar, of unlawful conduct in regards to this dispute, yet it was the victim of this treachery who was removed?! Further, farewell speeches were obviously agreed in advance for there was an allegation part of which was missing - did Oliver depart on his terms where this was deliberately changed but not in a manner in which he could address the discrepancy, again, due to the treachery of others? Only within a dictatorship could such be allowed to happen, unless there was more going on behind the scenes, such like my actions. The devious little bastard that I am...

There was much animosity but the Chief Constable maintained his, 'conscience was clear' (which appears accurate) and at one stage he threatened to take legal action against them that were savaging him. All this happened to remove a senior police officer just days earlier from what had been a long career, for his retirement dates had previously been announced! When that is considered the situation appears to be ludicrous in relation to the child murder it was purporting to be about.

In consideration of what happened here; a police Chief Constable was removed and the two most senior politicians in Scotland had question marks placed over their behavior with a third prominent Labour Councilor also displaying behavior that should, in any circumstances, have them all removed from Office. A second Police Chief Constable came under attack after these events happened, but calls for the resignation of the boss of Central Force were ignored. This case centered on the mass murder of schoolchildren by a crazed gunman at Dunblane, which could have more substance to it.

After all this, without doubt, I was certain I was the nemesis behind the farcical dispute having played them at their own game and won convincingly.

From my initial tactic of using the court proceedings in conjunction with the press, to others such as my 'Press release', vandalism, poster campaigns, sabotage, graffiti etc, these methods allegedly claimed a number of high profile victims yet I was still alive and at liberty to do it all over again. Every time I used a method and capitalized from it I then had to devise another way of confronting the corrupt system knowing that technique would soon be exhausted when the security forces acknowledged it. No terrorist using conventional methods could ever achieve such major results, or have such a long career before being apprehended, or *dealt* with. I operated solely by stealth never claiming what I'd done. Just silently watching what was mainly front-page news stories cover these exploits until a mistake brought me to the public's attention. My 'Press release' almost certainly instigated the rumpus that removed Grampian Chief Constable, Dr. Oliver, but it was the removal of the Strathclyde Chief Constable, John Orr, that exposed me to the larger public. The police Chief just announced an extension to his career then suddenly reverted to announcing his retirement shortly afterward leaving a massive contradiction for the public to pick up upon. At the time I'd been given the telephone number of the human rights group, *Liberty*, and asked if I would give them an outline of my story. When I did, the Police Chief announced his retirement within hours of making that call. Again, another nasty coincidence maybe, but rumors circulated I was responsible for his removal where now word was on the streets about someone capable of removing a police Chief Constable – if they only knew the truth with the irony to the overall situation! This interception could have come about because telephones I use have a habit of being tapped (voice recognition is a reality), although the call was made out with my vicinity. Otherwise, is a human rights organization being monitored by the Secret Service?

For all this, the most controversial event was the death of Donald Dewar whose status hadn't changed for years but his title had. When the Scottish Parliament reconvened after three hundred years of absence he was made First Minister. I held personal grievances against him such as him being accused of unlawful conduct when he acted to remove the Grampian Police Chief Constable fractionally early from his post but never answered to accusations made against him with the potential to find out if I'd been the real instigator in what definitely appeared to be a fabricated dispute. When I did my poster campaign his constituency was covered knowing my message would eventually find its way onto this politician's desk. Then, finally, I had another incident with the police just prior to his death that could also be brought to his attention. So in light of all this, in the week before he died I was told the exact words, "Donald Dewar will not be alive at the end of this week."

Two days later Dewar was in intensive care and then he died two days after. Four days after hearing this prediction! Obviously there was reason for it. Dewar was pressured into an early grave, alternatively, years later, in reconsideration the pressure may have come from darker sources... I was never updated on the event of his death - a traitor's death - though I always presumed it were natural causes irrespective of the prediction...

Once again, weighing up the various methods of fighting the corrupt system rarely are top politicians removed, although in this case natural causes were given for the official cause of death. Strange how a second version about the pressure he was subjected to immediately before his death should materialize from inside the Scottish Parliament. Was there a need to promote an ailing Dewar not coming under attack from myself? If I greatly contributed to his premature death, he only had himself to blame because I only acted to prevent the murder of fellow citizens. Could he, in his position of responsibility, honestly claim the same? Could he live with himself given the situation? He acted in opposition to me. Once deceased, his reputation was tarnished by the scandalous building costs of the new Scottish Parliament, which was claimed to be his pet project. It is doubtful he was solely responsible for the spiraling construction costs but at an inquiry many laid the blame on him; maybe it was too convenient to do this. A bronze statue erected in his honor was vandalized with, among other things, pink paint splattered around his buttocks. He'd been divorced for a long time then lived his remaining years without a known partner. Was this done to indicate he was a homosexual? Both attempts to sully his reputation were made after I named him on the internet in the scandal involving the Grampian Police Chief. Why was his reputation tarnished after his death? Was it because he was associated with murders of innocents he was supposed to protect and now needed to be distanced from the Labour Party to protect its image in disregard for justice and human rights?

Donald Dewar was succeeded as First Minister by Henry McLeish. From the day this happened I plotted McLeish's downfall. In contrast to police Chief Constables being removed where who I deliberately target are not what makes me known, this time there would be no doubt regarding my actions. Never an opportunity was missed to publicly state I believed McLeish was somewhat involved in the ongoing affair. Undeterred with the knowledge about the Brighton Bomber where no stone was left unturned in the hunt for him afterwards, I still persevered with tackling McLeish. If I were to actually attack such a senior politician the persecution would be unbearable, but I already lived under such circumstances therefore had less reason to feel threatened by repercussions. Where, in contrast to others being involved in similar antics, it could raise my profile making me more respected therefore less likely to suffer retribution. Self-confidence was bolstered by past events - mainly an incredible run of knocking out top officials one after another - and McLeish was just too irresistible a target. Thereby, I promised I would bring him down even if it killed me. It was an hour of death or glory once again.

In connection with the forthcoming incident, I was nearly killed. Was this done to save the career of this lackluster politician and with it the reputation of the Labour Party? His character deserves to be examined closely regarding how he behaved regarding a child murder, prostitute murders and what could be associated deaths, plus my attempted murder on this occasion!

Who I alleged to be Tracey Wilde's killer died the same day Henry McLeish fronted a television news article concerning the unemployed wherein was footage showing myself looking for employment inside a *Job Centre*. This is all undeniable and could possibly be part of a conspiracy to murder. As ever, to be in possession of incriminating information is one thing but to capitalize from it is an entirely different matter especially when the truth is being habitually stifled in Government related issues. My next tactic was to write a book naming McLeish in this event and allege his part in a greater conspiracy. From a personal point of view, it was therapeutic writing down past experiences having endured so much. The text described in detail circumstances surrounding the removal of the Grampian Police Chief and how my photocopied message most likely instigated the whole prolonged ill-fitting affair. This was all very damning and could ruin the career of the new First Minister. Writing such a book is the easy part, getting it published is extremely difficult because nobody wants to take such a risk because they may be sued due to the content. Publishers should have been less cautious in this instance, where it is doubtful what was written was ever going to be publicly debated in any court! There was little in the way of crimes against humanity and human rights violations the British Government were not accused of here. In the year 2001 the e-book was in its infancy so I decided I never needed a publisher but could have this story broadcast in this manner. The internet is free space, freedom of expression, therefore if the content is accurate I never needed to allege this or allege that but could write the truth without the same legal restrictions that exist in the conventional publishing industry. By accident and a combination of circumstances I ended up having one of the first e-books ever published.

I was extremely nervous dumping this work onto the internet knowing such a compilation could remove him where the authorities don't take lightly to such behavior. Just like the Brighton Bomber targeting Thatcher, it is a bit like suicide bombing such are the implications. But, in my favor another *coincidence* happened shortly after - the targeting of Scotland's First Minister, Henry McLeish! I was ecstatic knowing it would either be me or him that fell in a situation that wasn't going to be easily turned to my advantage. To begin with, he was secretly taped in private conversation with a fellow Minister calling a colleague, 'A patronizing bastard', which became front-page tabloid news. He claimed a microphone 'somehow' picked up this conversation, leaving speculation as to how this really occurred (were the Secret Service involved?). The dispute then went quiet but I would sporadically promote my website/e-book to his detriment just to keep the pressure on. The more damage I could do to his reputation at this point in time the more it favored my situation. A very sensible precaution given the circumstances! The reputation of the entire Labour movement was also at stake given what was occurring.

At the same time, all through the summer of 2001 I had legal proceedings pending with the police reluctant to release any statements in connection with this case. As the number of such dates ran into double figures finally it all came to a climax in October/November where this corresponded (another coincidence or most likely deliberately so?!) with a row blown up concerning McLeish's failure to register expenses for sub-letting of his constituency office. The trial date should have been the seventh of November 2001, but I was also failing to conform to the legal system therefore created a further delay. The trial date was once again postponed for another month, where it would have been nearly impossible to keep the dispute raging with McLeish in the public eye continue on for such a lengthy period of time so he was ousted the next day (another coincidence or most likely deliberately so?!). From the beginning of this fracas involving him, one commentator on national television news proclaimed, "There must be something else behind this."

Such a comment corresponded with what was going on behind the scenes. A commonly held opinion from the beginning was this First Minister could easily weather the storm. This is not what happened, which, again, questions the true motives behind his removal?!

In the end I never did stand trial but went on the run again to mysteriously find all charges dropped. A corrupt psychiatrist by the name of Dr. Locke was to give a second judgment on my mental health due to my corrupt lawyer asking the judge for such to derail the court case against me?! She previously found no mental deficiencies whatsoever, yet went on to fabricated medical reports to the contrary. However, she had completely overdone it. For what was written was preposterous in the extreme and downright absurd bearing no facet of reality. This was somebody that appeared to have no clients - and rightly so - obvious from the fact I had to wait over 45 minute after the appointment time in the surgery for her when it was empty! Plus, she brought up the predicament of a previous client in a similar position. What she never revealed was he committed suicide. His daughter said! This was at best a fool or at worst a dangerous fraudster British agents were using or manipulating to their advantage who should have had her license to practice revoked a long time ago! All of which can be fully substantiated with hard evidence to be beyond reasonable doubt!

Referring back to the legal proceedings; when you break all the rules and this is the outcome I can only put this down to the Scottish legal system being as corrupt as I presume it to be, or has demonstrated itself to be, with past incidents. Once again, what I viewed as a corrupt law worked in my favor yet never produced a verdict.

I have been found guilty every time I stood trial for whatever I was charged with previously. Going on the run is the only way I found of not being convicted when innocent of whatever I was accused of. Here, due to corrupt lawyers and a dubious psychiatrist, instead of receiving compensation for six fictitious charges plus injuries received, I could have been illegally detained in a mental institution?!

Incidentally, the damning e-book was entitled *'Who Killed Jill Dando'*. Those that edited this work gave it this title, which would attract attention given her celebrity and what at the time was an unsolved murder. Few people ever knew I was gambling on the fact by stating if my DNA was found inside Tracey Wilde's apartment the repercussions to which would fall on Henry McLeish. Such a tactic was successful. It was me who predicted and allegedly orchestrated the downfall of this high ranking official, and when it happened I said as a very happy man about those who doubted me, "And a million sad-cases went looking for rocks to hide under."

The world just found out this joker was for real irrespective of what they knew or what version of events they choose to accept! In retrospect, I had supposedly been rated the most dangerous man in Britain. Maybe now I was living up to this title with this and other exploits some of which had already came to the public's attention in selective exploits. People can look back at this episode in Scottish history and find two Police Chiefs and two First Ministers plus many others of high standing all removed under questionable circumstances! At the time it was all disguised by the media either not knowing what was happening or failing to broadcast the truth. Where, what they did convey never fitted with prevailing scenarios.

Was I really more powerful than the most senior politician in Scotland? He was removed when I said I would have him ejected. However, such probably only demonstrates his lack of authority in a land ruled by a dictatorship from the south. Coincidentally, the powers-that-be could never have him as a leading Labour politician once he was associated with a murder in the public eye, where it would have been the spooks who most likely removed him. This had been my intention all along. It was me who was now manipulating the corrupt system, playing them at their own game, and winning! For a final curious thought, why was he promoted when the security services were fully aware of what I knew with regards to my 'Press release'? Among other places, I sent a message directly to a Labour MP! Was this them rewarding him for his past cooperation thinking my actions could be contained concealed or discredited?

I really was playing with fire here, taking another massive gamble, when I needed to destroy the reputation and standing of the First Minister as a final precaution against being wrongfully convicted for the murder of Tracey Wilde. It worked! Not that he was ever investigated with the death of the Special Branch officer instrumental to this affair. Later on, there was talk of McLeish going to live and work in the United States, which is again curious given the setting. Were they planning to remove him out of the country hoping the accompanying stigmas left with him? Or, was it to prevent him being investigated at a later date (if a justice system is restored)? Or, did they fear I had more dirt to expose? The death in question that created this scenario could be the tip of an iceberg of mass murder, where, here was the Scottish Labour Party implicated in it all!

As for repercussions or containment; when I next returned home in April 2002 I was constantly being pursued by Customs and Excise, Special Branch and police until caught out on leaving a Labour Party Office (of all damned places)! I left that office intent on following the instructions given only to find myself under surveillance from undercover police then to be arrested shortly after for walking in a public park. At the time I was holding the headed note-paper from the Houses of Commons (British Parliament). Once again this could be regarded as tactics used in a dictatorship, especially when the under-cover personnel were removed from the complaint against me?! I cursed and called the Labour Party for everything imaginable. They'd been a pet hate for a long time prior to this happening for the pretense and false hope they give to the Scottish nation when betraying every principle they supposedly stand for. Now I was vehemently against them more than ever. No doubt they would feel my wrath in the future!

I was supposed to claim back four and a half years unemployment benefit but of course I never received a penny thanks to being caught out by this set-up. Once again, I was left questioning the situation where Labour Party, Secret Service and Strathclyde Police could have a vested interest in denying me this legitimate claim.

When I was arrested they extracted a DNA sample where with this I knew I could still be looking at thirty-five years in a prison cell for double murder - my word against that which could incriminate prominent Government Ministers in a legal system favoring them. You have to be realistic and accept that I, as an innocent man and a stone in the shoe of the British Establishment, was never going to see justice from such a corrupt situation. As ever, this is all but a smidgen away from the definition of a dictatorship, if not actually being one! The only thought I had at the time if I was to be wrongly convicted was to ask the judge for forty-five years because I had no pension fund anyway and may as well die in a prison cell. In the end all I could do was make a fuss about the situation then promptly leave never to return. On departing, I asked a friend for a gun, where if the police came calling I was going to leave them dead on the doorstep then make for Brazil such was my frame of mind, as I no longer had anything to lose, for I may as well be wanted/convicted for something opposed to being chased for frivolous reasons. By making that final stand, it could have been done in the hope of highlighting the problems imposed thereby potentially change things for the better. Although this friend always held some kind of firearm he declined to supply... In hindsight, I was probably too volatile at that stage to be holding anything dangerous and would have shot someone, most likely my half-witted brother for all the grief he caused. By now this fool was finally notable by his silence. I had suffered every misfortune imaginable at his hands. Although I was to be granted political asylum Switzerland never appealed to me and once again I sought sanctuary in the Republic of Ireland to be under constant surveillance of Irish Special Branch and MI5 once again.

From the European Union I had to find a country outside of which to be granted political asylum. All of this had already been discussed.

The pressure was now too much given what was endured where I spent the entire summer of 2002 only seconds away from being dead such was the actual pressure inside my head. Was it not for a friend and an accidental visit to Romania, which I found totally lawless therefore free of oppression, I doubt if I would ever have recuperated. On the streets of Bucharest two small explosions took place, but whatever was happening was paradise compared to the brutality of life in Scotland. Otherwise, it is always women who rescue me from my darkest hours, where I can still remember this cheeky little voice saying, "Hey Robert, we paint a picture."

Then she dragged me off to the art shop. Slowly I would recover where in the meantime some other innocent man was arrested for the murder of Jackie Gallacher solely to prevent my case being aired in the new Scottish Parliament – (falsified) legal proceeding now preceding. This is a consistent tactic of the police/security services. Tracey Wilde's murder was conveniently ignored. I had allegedly named and then broadcast a picture of her killer. These allegations possessed implications to both Strathclyde Police and the Labour Government so there was good reason for the authorities to ignore them, just like they do in some third world totalitarian regime. This is an apt description regarding the status Scotland has been reduced to. Maybe it was always this corrupt, with me too young to remember anything other than constant tyranny.

I could never understand the Freemasons on a personal level. Those I knew to be part of the brotherhood liked to pretend they were a force in society, a power to be reckoned with, but from experience this was never the case. They would give a nod and a wink after telling about how they were going to deal with a certain situation but their bluster never materialized into actions and they only looked silly at the outset. Why do they behave in this manner? Old men pretending they could still cut the mustard, when-I-was-a-lad, that type of thing. They only set themselves up for ridicule irrespective of the suspicion they already attract with their secretive nature. Where their influence lies is in the business world. Like, when a friend gave the company boss a Masonic handshake (in slang known as a knuckle-grinder) and became employed at a time when the company was no longer hiring staff. It was the only part of Masonic ritual he knew with him not being a member. How could these men ever think they could threaten me? None of them were ever brave enough as actually give a direct threat but convey their messages in a subtle manner thinking I would take heed. I, friends and associates are the ones who were not so full of shit, hence the brotherhood's caution in confronting me. If they knew their history, what they were supposed to protect, none of them would be qualified to make such insinuations. But; who am I to educate these deluded old men?

I wrote a second book giving the history of the Freemasons, in which it detailed out things like how the *Mother Lodge* is situated in the west of Scotland and how they were supposed to honor the Declaration of Arbroath, when it read:

'For, as long as but a hundred of us remain alive, never will we on any condition be brought to English rule.'

All Freemasons the world over are Scottish nationalists by definition, and became republicans from the year 1587 onwards (if they care to research the subject instead of portraying a misguided one-up-man-ship attitude). This book was critical of the Grand Lodge of England for changing principles and practices and then adopting a false position of British-ness, plus wrongfully supporting the present British Royal Family. To really poke the brotherhood in the eye with a sharp stick, I went out and took a photograph of the 'Pyramid Stone', which they claim marks the exact spot the embalmed head of Jesus Christ was brought to Scotland seven hundred years ago. Very few of them can find this landmark, but in typical fashion I could. Anything you are never meant to have your hands upon always seems to be in my possession. It is them who should be careful who they make muffled threats against. I might just ask them to honor their proposals! As for the book, it was never edited nor published.

To install a measure of humanity back into my life I also wrote a poem in keeping with the cultural aspect of events. What was written wasn't particularly nationalistic or inspirational but more of a personal saga. At the bottom, in brackets, I always wrote, *'Of the persecuted'* to highlight the inhumanity experienced. On a light-hearted note, I have yet to find a piece of historic writing from Ireland/Northern Ireland to copy in reverse of how Republican and Loyalist sympathizers manipulate the Declaration of Arbroath, neither have I painted a mural.

CALI.

I took the last train leaving, thinking of cherry eyes,
Stood there alone believing, her beauty would pass me by,

Soul wretched and tormented, leaving the station,
Here's whining steel in motion to some unknown destination,
For runners run and gunners gun but the devil ne'er got me,
Ten thousand miles of empty tracks and breaking hearts knowing I'd be free,
But through it all there is but one motto worth obeying,
In French, 'red and black, red and black' Cali is a saying,
Today I wouldn't have you back, selling cherries in Marseille.

I felt my old heart bleeding, dreaming of cherry eyes,
Separated and forsaken, knowing I'd surely die,
Sold out by your treason, curse of our nation,
He who fought them to a man then dreamed of liberation,
For traitors ill and cowards won then sore was the day,
When they marched them down to London town for medals and better pay,
Cursed by the few I give you a motto worth obeying,
In French, 'red and black, red and black' Cali is a saying,
Today I wouldn't have you back, selling cherries in Marseille.

I took the last post 'n' chorus, singing of cherry eyes,
In the ground they'll lower us, under some foreign sky,
So let this be lamented, rising again,
Steely eyed and determined to run my race against them,
For what is done and what'll come the just' will never be,
You telling of the Promised Land in foreign hands for greed and tyranny,
Red and black and red and black and now you're free of me,
Red and black and red and black but that will never be,
Today I wouldn't have you back, selling cherries in Marseille.
(Of the persecuted.)

The adage about the harder the life the sweeter the song may apply here...

Whoever *Cali* was remained a mystery, for I never said. Was it a girl's name, the Greek God of war, a shortened version of Caledonian, which was the old Romans gave for Scotland, or, all of the above? Maybe it was the name of the local pub! All I ever explained was the *devil* was the British Government but the rest remained mysterious – probably because I didn't know either! The song was popular for all its ambiguous nature. Beforehand, when on the run in Portugal, I would recite poetry just to while away the hours with little money and no companions to provide any form of entertainment.

On a side-note, Bobby Sands is credited with writing the popular Irish folk song *'Wish I was back home in Derry'*. With Sands from Belfast (Derry being the common name for the city of Londonderry), I always wondered if he was the actual author or if he assisted someone with the lyrics when being an inmate of the Maze Prison.

What was learnt from all that transpired is everyone in Scottish society was expendable to the British Establishment. No living person there was safe from their injustices when the aims fitted the need. Politicians could be removed, which is an affront to democracy vindicating the fact it is rule by dictatorship. Rank and file police officers, prison wardens and Special Branch agents were mere cannon fodder and even big-wigs such as police chiefs could be attacked and disposed of, but only if you knew how. At the time I was crazed enough, or condemned enough, to attempt to confront all before me. Where the real power lay was in England. London has the Houses of Parliament, MI5 and MI6 headquarters and Buckingham Palace. Cheltnam has the electronic eves dropping center GCHQ. Porton Down is a biological weapons laboratory. And; in the county of Herefordshire the SAS are stationed. These were the untouchables.

Basically, strategy upon accepting the media didn't exist in its correct and accepted form for a democracy or the law was just a charade to benefit the privileged few was to ignore both and find alternative ways of challenging the tyranny presented. The prevailing situation was one of the most impossible imaginable with the Men in Black operating, a multitude of suspicious deaths, and the framing of innocent people for murder, but it needed challenging. Challenge it I did with unique methods and tactics creating a barrage of problems for the authorities to cover

over. Even when the cracks started appearing they continued as before, albeit weakened and frustrated. Slowly they would become more alienated from the general public, but I ran out of time to attack them thus far to completely alienate them. From this, I was only left wondering just how many arms did they have to twist to cover things up? And; how many favors did they call in to deceitfully preserve their (despicable) image? Timing was equally critical when holding so little in the way of resources opposing ridiculous forces. I was forever running around in circles confusing everybody, twisting this way then that so the truth or real intention could never be surmised. U-turns in direction and strategy were frequent where sometimes objectives were made up on-the-wing because it wasn't possible to fulfill an original objective. It could be done once the right methods were found and the correct attitude adopted. I did and succeeded. Not that I ever seen it that way, just ploughing on regardless searching for the next target or opportunity. Most of the time these exploits were purely about survival, and from the two basic facts I was still alive and at liberty this is a real indication of true success. I was highly rated yet untouchable. Maybe it was all just a game where the last man standing is the winner – Russian roulette-esque. Adversaries fell one after another whereas I was left standing, and defiant!

'God damn them all, we'd buy no guns, shed no tears.'

4. PUBLICITY AND PROPAGANDA.

'*Your man was a sailor, he was not a gangster, but when they needed someone to sail the boat, he was right for the job. He was under no illusion the cargo would be illegal and inevitably it all ended in tears with him left lying in prison. One of the gang members turned supergrass during the trial, which peeved the gang leader, who in turn put £40,000 out on his head.*
Once out of jail, this sailor asked me, "What would do to someone for £40,000? There are two conditions."
Upon knowing who was really behind this, after repeated, "I don't want to know about this."
He coaxed me into answering his question. A reluctant reply being, "One, you kill him and two, you kill his family."
A shake of the head, "No, nothing barbaric like that. One; you find him, and two; he is still alive when HE gets there."
HE in question was the gang leader and who I always regarded as the godfather of Scottish crime. This incident happened in the mid nineteen-eighties but no one really knew who HE was. Newspapers at the time promoted old Arthur Thomson as the Glasgow godfather - a claim I always disputed. Back then, a contract out on someone's life was priced around £2,000 (this being prior to drug money hiking up the price exponentially) but here was someone placing twenty times that amount as a bounty – crime would never be the same again. The media provided the cover for a new wave to materialize, a super league, without the general public knowing it was here.'

When the Provisional IRA was first formed, there were questions regarding a Protestant element. Such could be to their advantage for being solely Roman Catholic meant they excluded a large portion of the Irish community, and with which their support. In contrast to this situation, a personal story could have made their so called *war* winnable. This entailed giving them an essential Protestant influx. Back in the nineteen-seventies a relative had an unusual enterprise. He went around farms of Ayrshire buying up old firearms at a time when regulations regarding guns were lax compared to today's stringent standards. Farmers at that period would have an array of shotguns at their disposal, few of which registered. Such a practice was a throwback from the Second World War where the countryside was left littered with unaccounted for weapons. Where, back in the day, it was not uncommon for poachers to go fishing using explosives creating new pools in the river as they went! This relation then went over to Ireland to sell what was collected for a healthy profit. So who was buying? At the time Protestant Loyalist terror groups were not well established, and those that were had many allegations of collusion with the British Army and the other security forces operating there, which in the circumstances would most likely make weapons (illegally) available to them. This, by deduction, made the most likely recipients of his guns the freshly emerging Provisional IRA who were embarrassingly short of firepower in those formative years.

An interesting story maybe, but it was only later did an uncle talk either of this relative or his brother as being, "The only person I have ever known to have been thrown out of the Orange Lodge."

Where he maintained, "They throw no one out of the Orange Lodge."

With which, he could never account for what lay behind this unusual action.

When the British forces of law and order discover someone acting on behalf of, or with, a terrorist group they do not always arrest them immediately. No; what they do is keep them under surveillance for a period of time to try to discover who else is involved in the operation in any possible larger network and also to ascertain a background assessment on them. The more information they can collect the easier it is to secure a conviction, or as a means of bribery to turn them against their own. Likewise, it is to the security forces benefit to discover others who may not be known of. What would happen if they found a member of the staunchly Protestant Orange Lodge supplying weapons to the staunchly Catholic Provisional IRA at a critical time when they had to be seen being solely Roman Catholic to prevent further Irish and international support amassing? An arrest could result in a criminal trial where the defendant would be exposed to public scrutiny revealing he was part of the most revered Protestant institution of the day. Tabloid newspapers would have a printing bonanza uncovering such a revelation. Security forces could never afford the propaganda coup such a trial would hand to the Provisionals, therefore they would do all within their power to frustrate it taking place. So what were the options open to them other than to ignore him altogether hoping - probably knowing given how matters were heading - his operation would soon run its course to finalize quietly? This was at a time before allegations of shoot-to-kill policies were prevalent. The only answer to the predicament would be to have the gunrunner ostracized, in particular, by exclusion from the Orange Lodge. By doing so he would cease his activities with a minimum of public knowledge. In the end his business would become irrelevant, where, as the nineteen-seventies turned into the eighties the Provisionals became more sophisticated in armory with supplies coming in from Libya. Given which, old shotguns and occasional out-of-date rifles this relative could acquire would soon become of no consequence to the situation in Northern Ireland. His Irish contacts could also be exposed by means of surveillance for intelligence gathering with no direct interference in his dealings! The fact remains, publicity can influence judicial matters before a trial materializes, but not always in the obvious *verdict sense*.

Another example of publicity being manipulated, in a personal scenario, was when I had a need to alleviate the pressure I lived under, therefore decided to create a diversion. England had never played against Scotland at soccer for the last ten years and when they did this was the opportunity I was waiting for. For certain, this was one in which I was not going to pass up on! In the past there had been violence between supporters, with the most famous occasion being at Wembley Stadium back in 1979 when the Scots invaded the pitch and then hung from the goal-posts until they broke. They also dug up the pitch to take home with them, where, those caught with Wembley turf on the train home they often joked with the police, 'My brother-in-law is away on holiday and asked me to look after his garden for him!' It was time for me to stage a terrorist uprising, Scotland against England. A need was there, especially so when my life depended upon it... British football is notorious for its violence so as I plotted an attack, what were the options? Who would I fight rival fans with? And, with what weapons could be used? When sitting there contemplating strategy I realized even if I put a hard cell of men together - a real death or glory brigade, i.e. the nut-jobs in society - we would still be defeated due to England having a greater number of fans-cum-thugs to crush our resistance. Never one to think along conventional lines this *army* could comprise of thugs, gangsters, Legionnaires and British Army soldiers. It was important to have serving British soldiers in the gang just to annoy the Secret Service if we got arrested - watch them squirm in embarrassment when they try to ostracize their own with the press being fed statements like, 'It was completely out of character of him...'

My thinking may have been good but the plan was beset with problems other than a lack of numbers and having to pay recruits to fight at a time when I was bankrupt, plus, a final consideration being what weapons to use. If it was overdone someone could end up dead and then there would be no hiding place for whoever was involved after the confrontation. I can remember being at a local riot, when after, being accused of running away. I did, and admit it without shame, for I was the only person there that wasn't armed, and so I had ran around the front of the building to lift two bricks for defense. From that incident, with the level of violence entailed, I knew how easy it was to go too far. The next day a First World War bayonet was found in the van I was driving that night. Of the blade's fifteen inch length (in a star profile) twelve inches were covered in blood - human blood (where, after a period of hiding it in case there was anything serious to answer to, I returned it to its owner).

The time had come to think differently about the scenario. It was time to think my way. In this position, I needed that terrorist outbreak badly but it had to be done in such a manner the security forces would never suspect me of being involved. At the time I lived under almost twenty-four hour surveillance so it was not going to be easy to dupe them. Then again, what is the point of not doing it if you cannot pull it off right under their noses without them knowing? There will always be that element of defiance leading me to undermine every initiative made to contain my actions.

 The number of men I could gather may be low, but, did I need them? There are always alternatives when fighting rival English. Maybe my father's and grandfather's history lessons came to be fore when they claimed the Scots were always out-numbered in past victories against the *Auld Enemy*. And; where would I attack them? Not in the obvious battlefield arena of Glasgow where violence was expected to erupt beside the football stadium but in a location of my choosing. Casuals – smartly dressed football fans intent on causing trouble – met in Edinburgh to fight. Obviously, they were thinking similar thoughts. A surprise attack of an unpredictable nature it would be. Again, Scots, in times gone by, always chose the lie of the land to favor them in the cases where they fought. I was no longer looking for a fight but an isolated guerrilla attack, just like back in the good old days - aka William Wallace!

 The more I considered it, the more I realized the country didn't need a few thousand English football thugs roaming the streets, causing violence and destruction here, and so I would do the country a favor and *cut them off at the border,* this being to prevent them from entering Scotland thereby keeping rival supporters in their country. One-day the people might have the decency to thank me for all the things I did for them... All the misery I spared them of without them ever knowing it?! Not to mention all the lives I saved...

 To do this, I simply needed to know how rival fans were entering the country. The answer was mostly by road and train. Otherwise, a limited few with money flew in. Road traffic is a difficult proposition to stop due to the versatility of the car combined with various alternative routes available, particularly so, when the influx was over a period of several days. Airplanes are nearly impossible to disrupt without horrific consequences (at this stage I was probably crazed enough as attempt to take an airplane out of the sky if I possessed the means, where, years later I had MI5 growling at me for a helicopter falling out the sky but I was never involved, for it resulted from a bum pilot). Trains are a different proposition, because they are restricted to a few select lines without the potential to deviate onto other routes. Not only that, modern trains are electric therefore easier to halt compared to past diesel powered versions with an independent power source that can chug on through fire and high water. Now instead of directly attacking a train full of crazed-up football supporters all I needed to do was bring it to a halt, have it left stationary for a lengthy period of time, whereby the mostly drunk stoned and high men inside would soon become frustrated if they thought they were never going to get to the expected destination. Such a scenario raises the possibility of them to start fighting amongst themselves. The train could implode in these circumstances! Genius never fails me...

My actions went unnoticed, no publicity or anything like that to say what had happened. Nothing at all! I doubted my success. That being, until the two sides were about to play a return match in England a few weeks later. Just prior to the Scots traveling south there were media reports railway carriages were set on fire in Scotland, which was claimed might prevent Scots reaching Wembley Stadium. Very interesting, I thought. The original attack never made the headlines - alternatively, if it did, I never seen it when constantly looking for them - but here is another incident involving the rail network extensively broadcast?! So what was happening here?

If the authorities had a terrorist outbreak without knowledge concerning those behind it - certain it was not me such is the ridiculous levels of surveillance I live under - they would stage their own little debacle to use as a means of telling the unknown guilty party to cease their activities. The message being delivered from such; it may prevent their side going to the big return match. Basically, a warning to whoever was responsible for the original attack was they were hurting their own. With control over the media the genuine incident could be kept quiet (by putting out a D-notice) but they could promote their bogus event of burning old and redundant railway carriages solely for propaganda purposes. The press in Scotland is no longer free to allow such manipulation.

The above scenario could be viewed in reverse with the next incident presented: An older relation sat beside me in the car far removed from his vicinity in rural countryside when he witnessed a shooting-party. A rag-tag bunch of friends and acquaintances appeared out of the undergrowth from nowhere heavily laden down with guns, all dressed in combat fatigues and survival accoutrements. Even to have known all present, they, in my opinion, looked like Hell's rejects that had just been offered £50 to the first one who could shoot his grandmother dead. Where it has to be asked; how would this motley crew look to an outsider? It defies definition?! Now I honestly never knew what they were going to shoot; who they were about to shoot; nor, was I about to ask in case I found myself the wrong end of a fire-stick! Alternatively, as it has been known, they could end up shooting each other just for the hell of it. On sighting the characters involved I knew not all of whom would hold a gun license. Some may have had to sign the *Firearms Act*, which, from other sources not present that day, stated they would get an automatic five years in prison just for being in possession of any firearm - loaded or unloaded! This source spoke from first-hand experience so without checking the details I took his word at face value.

So, in these circumstances, best I ask this relation to keep quiet with a congenial; "That never happened; agreed?!"
"Agreed."
"Thanks."

With his word upon it off we drove with a change of subject hoping never to hear about it again, or of the outcome of the day's shooting... It soon became apparent he never kept shtum when another relation later started inquiring about an *army* I knew of roving about the countryside.

"How many of them support Celtic?"

This was being asked to determine if the group was a Scottish based Irish nationalist gang on training exercises.

"Most of them are Glasgow Rangers supporters as far as I know; others I don't think they care either way. Few of them support Celtic."

Said in honest reply to appease his questioning. In doing so it left the assumption they were an underground army of Scottish nationalists getting ready for an uprising. Another acquaintance, also distant from where the group was sighted, later on eagerly told of underground Scottish militias forming in my vicinity. Initially, I never knew what he was talking about, but hints and allegations told of two or three groupings of paramilitaries twenty to thirty strong heavily armed in training getting ready to overthrow the British Government. I was listening to this being said in all seriousness not realizing the original grouping was being exaggerated, and then taken out of context to treble in number and distort the status of. Rumor fueled rumor around round the country about militias in training... an attack being days away... support was rising... numbers were increasing by the day... where news of which obviously filtered back to the British Secret Service. Where, although, one source was blabbing the next was keeping tight-lipped about his contacts thereby complicating the overall scenario. So in a panic the press (as a propaganda service) were used imaginatively again with articles writing about militias in the west of Scotland (at the time adding in Fife in the east so not to identify direct sources) getting ready to launch an attack?!

What actually transpired was the spooks were hearing rumors but were unable to track those involved (Hell's rejects) down, therefore were appealing to the general public through the media in an attempt to find rebels that never existed?! For a final word on this; them from a nationalist perspective, upon hearing these stories, became full of anticipation where it exerted a desire for an uprising to right the wrongs being committed in the crippled status of the west of Scotland whereas British Government forces exerted a desire to quell and continue the oppression by force of arms if necessary. In history, the overall scenario was reminiscent of Jews living under Roman occupation at the time of Jesus when anxiously waiting for the Messiah to appear to liberate them. Any hint of an uprising being eagerly anticipated. I would find out later the oppressors were heavily Jewish influenced - insulting as it is!

There had already been my tactic of using publicity from the court case but nothing was ever so damning as the 'Press release'. What happened after that was either Government Ministers conspired in giving out a warning to halt further leaks where the content of the message was catastrophic to them involved because it named an alleged murderer fully implicating Government agents, or, there was a genuine dispute with the Grampian Police Chief ill-defined in the extreme. Even Chief Constable Oliver at the time of his forced removal publicly questioned the true motives regarding the abusive nature of the ongoing dispute. Either way the press had access to a story that was one of the most scandalous in recent times yet never followed it up. Whatever happened to investigative journalism? Nowadays reporters just trot out the given version of events, the party line so to speak, without looking for the truth, especially so in Scotland where free speech, human rights and laws are secondary to British Government requirements.

Other examples of a tyrannical regime undermining free speak sometimes belie the truth. During the Cold War, in the West there was no shortage of allegations as to what the KGB were accused of. Even a wet summer in England could be blamed upon too many Russian satellites in the sky (in the late eighties this was being said?!). Global warming was not a popular catchphrase then nor did they consider records of past climates when relaying this nonsense. You look back on it now and wonder just what complete and utter fools they made out of the general public. Not that it ever ceased in present times. They just changed the agenda but not the tactics. When the Berlin Wall fell (1988) it became less favorable to blame former Communists thereafter for all the ills in the world. No it wasn't, but an alternative bad guy quickly materialized to haunt the Western world. He became known as the Russian Mafia.

A quick explanation about this may be helpful to the uninformed. The secret police in many former Communist countries retained power once Communism collapsed by using and abusing their positions of influence and contacts to exploit the newly emerging Capitalist system. In Eastern Europe, many former spies can be seen driving expensive European cars with blacked-out windows – Mafia style. From what transpired, there is no unity of a Russian Mafia but gangs that developed locally without a national collectivity to them, therefore accusing them as a single entity leaves the blame running around looking for someone else to pin itself onto. Conveniently so, when they are falsely accused of something! Finally, like any Mafia or gang, being of a criminal nature no one wants to step forward and accept responsibility for whatever they are accused of. This is all too convenient if it is being used to fool the ignorant masses in the West. When I first went to Croatia I couldn't believe how relaxed it was after years of spiteful reporting – war, ethnic cleansing, oppression and Communism. I also couldn't explain what I was doing there. When asked, I maintained I went there to buy a pair of socks; nice socks they were!

Other than one famous story told to me direct from a croupier about how a casino in the Baltic States swindled an English business-man with the aid of electronic surveillance at the card table when the lady playing had a large ring on a finger that was in fact a miniature camera, and, one of her earrings was a speaker where both were controlled with background assistance. Her trick was to pass cards face down over the ring...

The allegedly KGB assisted Russian Mafia originally, by and large, traded in women (for prostitution and marriage), guns, employment and protection rackets but little else. Drugs became a more recent development. Just like it did for other Western gangs. I have the benefit of seeing how they operate first-hand, so when stories blaming them for other crimes outside their remit crop up it develops cynicism. The murder of celebrity Jill Dando, as an example, had the Russian Mafia as belated suspects. A first-class fantasy about a spurned Russian gangster aided by IRA hit-men - reality being, the IRA would go looking to hire Russian hit-men and not vice versa! By this stage I'd heard of their supposed involvement in awkward crimes that didn't fit their capabilities once too often, which left me with the thought, 'Not the Russian Mafia again!'

In light of this, it was a local example that intrigued me more than any other supposed Russian Mafia crime, because some friends knew the victim. When the known Glasgow gangland character Stewart 'Specky' Boyd was killed when his car burst into a fireball in Spain, accusations became rife about this accident being a murder where a bomb caused the explosion. Different suspects were proposed suggesting who was responsible for whatever different reason. The most fascinating to materialize was, you guessed it, the ill-fitting Russian Mafia.

A newspaper story claimed they had blown up Boyd's car, killing him, his daughter, a friend and a young girl in retaliation for a cocaine deal that went wrong. The Russian Mafia operates in Spain but cocaine (back then) was not a great source of their activities. In fact, as most people know, cocaine comes from the other side of the world (Central and Southern America). The Latin connection and shared language ideally have Spaniards in a position to deal with South Americans. Whoever made up this story failed to take that into account to make it sound realistic, which begs the question; who are the fictitious Russian Mafia that continually appear taking the blame for crimes that patently aren't theirs? Were the authors of the story relying on the fact Spain has serious amounts of cocaine – many different dealers and smugglers - which would, again, make this story more difficult to substantiate or disprove?

Did Stewart Boyd have something in his past to provide the answer? He was accused of many things including threatening Labour MP Irene Adams. Where, from personal circumstances, I've known for a long time the British authorities don't take lightly to the targeting of politicians, especially their favored unionist politicians (in contrast, opposition nationalist politicians suffer at their hands). The other Russian Mafia case sharing a personal interest to myself was Jill Dando. Where, with her being a celebrity this automatically qualified the lady to be under Secret Service surveillance. Furthermore, Dando had other reasons to be watched by the authorities (none of which were revealed by the media or at the trial, where had this happened it could have cast doubt on the verdict, especially when somebody of low intellect, most definitely not capable of this sophisticated crime, was convicted of her murder). When you consider both cases, the Russian Mafia appears closer to home than the British authorities care to admit! Those same authorities who previously never missed a trick in giving their alleged KGB forerunners a bad name...

The source of the Jill Dando tale was given as the Israeli Secret Service, Mossad. In recent years most Intelligence agencies around the world co-operate hand-in-hand. Only a handful of hostile countries refuse to share intelligence or provide false intel to assist another nationality's agency.

On a point of interest; it is standard British Army sabotage procedure to blow up cars by altering the elements within the car with electricity and gasoline present as the basis for an explosion! When this technique is applied there is little forensic evidence apparent in the aftermath from the fireball engulfing the car to prove conclusively what happened. Without divulging details of which, I know what to do and was taught this method by a former British Army soldier.

In 1948, George Orwell, wrote the book *1984* on the Scottish Island of Jura. His work is now considered a classic because of the way in which it predicts the future with his vision becoming an increasing reflection on modern life. Today, most people are familiar with the concept of *big brother is watching you* due to the introduction of surveillance cameras in public places. But, would Orwell ever have predicted another event on this quiet island to question modern society?

At a time when a Chinese satellite was predicted to re-enter the Earth's atmosphere a suspicious bush fire developed on Jura. On the night in question, I was leaving the city of Glasgow on the Hillington stretch of the M8 motorway with hundreds of other motorists traveling in the direction of Glasgow Airport when I noticed something fall out of the sky. A line of vision was such that this lime green light, coming down at a seven O'clock angle, would put it at the far side of the airport, or, if it was further in the distance, it would be over the mountains of the Mull of Kintyre thereby placing it in direct line with Jura. Perception is difficult to gauge at night given the distances referred to with darkness providing no pointers/landmarks to judge from. A larger object such as a satellite, placed further in the distance than excepted, would appear closer than it was due to the general assumption nothing oversize could fall to Earth from an airplane. Human psyche is conditioned in such a manner where it is unprepared to accept any other explanation. Personally, I never thought too much about an object falling out of the sky near an airport, other than the fact it was quite prominent. Contrary to the perception, flight is not the secure means of transport we are led to believe.

Now other people would never have given the incident a second thought or never tallied the two individual incidents together was it not for the claim made in the press there was a bush fire on the Island of Jura in January! Someone was having a laugh when this was printed. To get bracken to burn in this location at that time of year requires a very flammable spirit or an immense source of heat – like the inferno of a satellite burning up upon re-entering Earth's atmosphere! As kids, when we made fire-bombs to set wet bracken on fire I can remember my hand being alight with the petroleum spirit spilled onto it but still the vegetation never burned! At best all that would happen was the sodden plants would singe without actually igniting. This will give you a better indication about the wet Scottish climate and its effect on any January bush fire on a remote island.

Did this piece of propaganda hint at an even larger conspiracy? Why were we being denied the truth on this occasion? What caliber of journalist prints fairytales like these?

What exactly did former American President Ronald Regan refer to in a Star Wars program? A healthy diet of sci-fi has us all imagining laser beams coming down out the sky to knock out rival nuclear missiles when they are fired at the United States during a nuclear attack. This, at the time, is fantasy, because the energy required for such would be impossible to produce over any distance to make this prospect feasible. Alternatively, that Chinese satellite fell to earth a few years before the September the Eleventh plane crashes when the United States began promoting a new bogey man in the world post-Cold War once the Russians were considered friendly. Their new poltergeist was the Chinese...

Such begs the question; is it psychological conditioning or what that the United States always has a need to promote a bad guy in the world? Is this done so they can abuse all acceptable standards and violate all international laws without coming under suspicion themselves? Or, is it to detract from their failings?

Interesting; more interesting was the fact that after September the Eleventh the Chinese were not included in George W Bush's axis of evil. Did we miss something here in these days of New World Order? Countries included were Iran, Iraq and North Korea, with hints others such as Syria and Somalia were being considered, yet it was Afghanistan that was first attacked, where in doing so the subject of China went silent! Maybe the refusal to include China was not the only piece of hypocrisy attached to this list. After the planes hit the World Trade Center, Libyans offered the Americans help with their national disaster. The same Americans that supposedly murdered Colonel Gadaffi's step-daughter were now being offered Libya's assistance - Gadaffi, in fact, was playing them at their own game for she survived and worked in the hospital, as I heard from Libyan diplomatic sources! Or, what about the Syrians prior to the recent war who demanded Americans stop being hostile towards them or they would expose CIA operations within the country?! What a raw deal they were receiving, assisting the US on one hand yet being condemned on the other. Double standards attached were quite appalling. Of course it is, if it is true the American *Patriot Act* to take away the rites of ordinary citizens was written before those planes hit?!

To knock out satellites is an easier accomplishment than most would expect. It is more difficult keeping them within orbit of the Earth than it is to lose them. By simply altering their course, a satellite is either going to go away from Earth to be lost in the cosmos, or, if it is directed towards this planet it will burn up in the atmosphere. Either way it is gone forever with little or no evidence to say what happened. There will only be a limited period of transmission to detect any interference before total loss is accomplished. In recent times, gadgets have been developed to attack the satellites of other nations. Is this what Star Wars really is? Did the Americans attack the Chinese above our heads without our knowledge? Was Star Wars being fought pre-September the Eleventh? After which, was there a need to pacify the Chinese? Hence their non-inclusion in the hypocritical 'axis of evil'?! It was the United States of America that bombed the Chinese embassy in Belgrade in 1999 during the war there in a grave infringement of international law. This incident didn't sound particularly accidental with the allegation a total of three missiles were fired at the building!

Had China, as the original target for American vile propaganda, been added to George W Bush's list countries targeted they could have united and defeated the United States in a third World War. Scary! Instead, his coalition forces used to attack Iraq suffered greatly at the hands of their adversaries – the Iraqi insurgents have been more successful than what Western news agencies like to reveal. Such is the propaganda of war. What would it have happened if China assisted Saddam Hussein and the resurgent's?

None of these questions would ever have arisen had the press not tried to hoodwink the population with its bush fire – no pun intended.

When I was in the Cumnock workshop the SNLA terrorists frequented prior to their arrest, they once joked about shooting up the satellite tracking station in the hills to the south of the town. Fearful of the international consequences they declined. Instead, they targeted power lines for inconvenience to the general population achieving limited publicity. Had they attacked the station they would most likely have received less publicity but achieved more of a victory because it would have went to the heart of the Intelligence community. It is possible such an affront would never have seen print such is the restrictive nature of the Scottish 'free' press. Moreover, it could be to the terrorists benefit to disrupt a satellite tracking program, for it can be used against them. Likewise, had they done this their persecution would increase accordingly.

On the subject of American propaganda in both Afghanistan and Iraq the respected Arab news agency, Al-Jazeera, took direct hits from American forces in Kabul and Bagdad. Pre-Gulf War (2003) the company gave out the co-ordinates of its station within the city to prevent such an incident occurring again after the deadly experience in Kabul. The laser guided missiles that did the damage rely upon such co-ordinates for guidance, but the American military insist these were accidents. Many other journalists were also killed by coalition forces in Iraq. Some of whom were murdered at very strategic times. Afghanistan on the other hand is an inhospitable landscape plagued by warring factions and of less interest to the West, therefore had less media personnel present to cover the wars that occurred there. What these attacks did was reduce the capacity for an independent news broadcast from both conflicts with the world mainly being fed American orientated news bulletins afterward. Such like; why did all those American helicopter gunships suffer 'mechanical failure' yet none of them were actually shot down by rivals!? Perhaps; inventive journalism? Furthermore, in the Bosnian conflict the broadcasting station in Belgrade took a direct hit. Disturbing as it sounds, but even to the casual observer a pattern emerges here!

With infringements of the Geneva Convention concerning prisoners of war, the United States has a lot to hide in Iraq! What happened in Abu Ghraib Prison with the torture and sexual abuse of prisoners was only the tip of the iceberg concerning war crimes being committed by Allied forces in Iraq, if the information I have is accurate. Even the parading of Saddam Hussein on Western television is an infringement of the Convention because no POW can be used for propaganda purposes – Saddam was shown to the world in a type of, 'tell the world that we are winning' scenario. It was unsuccessful, where upon his arrest Iraq turned into a second Vietnam for the Americans where after Iraqis organized marches in support of Saddam! Maybe the reasons for going to war were all just bullshit, as Americans like to say, when the original reason for attacking Iraq changed from the supposed threat Saddam posed with his non-existent weapons of mass destruction to ridding the world of a supposed evil dictator. Where did the United States find the mandate to violate international law and human rights?

We all known Iraq was an oil war; don't we? Fictional weapons of mass destruction were just a front to steal the nation's oil wealth. Most go along with such, but having lived a life in the extremities of society I often get given a different perspective on events, especially here as there is no oil reserves to be stolen in the duplicity of the Afghanistan conflict?! Here is what they are really after, pre-flood (or Atlantain) technology! You don't swallow that? Well, the Garden of Eden was found exactly where the Bible said it is in the land of Cush, that being Hindu Cush Afghanistan. From which, they are looking at it not as some kind of paradise here on Earth, but as a genetics farm where man was first created - believe what you like...

The truth is all methods of communications are thwarted today. On becoming an internet warrior - a laughable suggestion given my life - but not wanting to be one of those sad-cases sitting alone in their underpants angrily spouting bile at the world but as someone with real revelations to be aired, so I joined a Scottish newspaper forum. It never lasted. After the Scottish referendum for independence - rigged beyond belief, if, like, those living in Scotland really wanted to stay part of a corrupt Union whose British forces are illegally murdering them (like turkeys voting for Christmas) - prominent SNP member Fiona Hyslop then after was briefed by Conservative Scottish leader David Mundell (someone who is an integral part of the British Establishment). I pointed this out and her ongoing suspicious actions only to find myself cut off from the forum! I was only asking who her actual sources were. For Mundell would have been briefed by British Intelligence, or, she was briefed by British Intelligence then using Mundell as a cover for such?!

For an example of what is occurring; the press would print a story such like thirty Glasgow drug addicts being killed in a weekend with Anthrax poisoning their heroin, but never investigate it. Glasgow is a small community given the right contacts. There were two main suppliers of heroin, both of whom got locked up at the same time, yet the amount of drugs thereafter that flooded into the city multiplied tenfold! A media report had two Scottish smugglers caught with heroin where both claimed they were working for MI6. Given all this, when, what is in essence, a mass murder occurs (ongoing!) the press deviate by creating the argument the poison was not confirmed being Anthrax allowing the killings to continue by diverting people's attention!

For all the media manipulation, and the affront to democracy it really is, sometimes it plays in my favor. The press, to maintain a readership, has to cover current events including deaths and resignations of top officials where I could be instrumental in such having removed many of them. When an event damning to the British Government occurs it would feature as an article where at the same time I would find myself under increased surveillance – such like there being three cars parked up near where I live that day/s instead of the usual one. Alternatively, if the article only featured in one newspaper it would sell out very quickly locally so I could not obtain a copy. From which, I would know to look for the corresponding news article or event to react to it... Basically, they were discreetly tipping me off with their actions unknown to them?!

In reverse of which; immediately before my first act in confronting the murderous regime I first checked with a local lawyer that I did have a legitimate defense of victimization, then after I came across another puzzling incident possibly related. Charles McGregor once stood trial for the murder of his wife, a working prostitute, but was acquitted. Where, that same night on the weekend days before the court appearance, I came across a young Special Branch officer looking in a dreadful state, to think to myself if anybody had just taken part in a murder when lacking the guts for it this scenario fitted perfectly here with him. In reverse of the ongoing practice; I then searched the newspapers just after to find the death of McGregor. In the article it was being overly hastily covered up with 'no suspicious circumstances' (a common statement and practice) printed as it was in black and white, because an original allegation against the mass murder of innocents was them who they failed to wrongfully convict of murder were then themselves murdered - this was fitting having had my visit from the SAS several months previous.

'If you tell a lie often enough, people will start to believe it.'

5. THE GREATEST ACT.

'One night I was drinking in a Glasgow bar when the company separated with the girls all sitting around a table and a mate going to talk to two heavies who'd just came in the front door, which left me alone at the bar in the company of a stranger. I had become fairly famous/infamous due to past events. This man, who was probably waiting for the opportunity, struck up a conversation addressing me by my nickname. "I hear you've had a bit of soapy-bubble, Chubby."
(Soapy-bubble is trouble from Cockney rhyming slang.)
Not wishing to give too much away I nonchantly replied "I've had my fair share."
He continued, "What are you going to do about it?"
"Me? It will be a chainsaw job." Bravado from too much beer.
"You're a man close to my own heart. You're talking to the man who did the chainsaw job." This being how he concluded.
My interest intensified, up until this point he was just another drunk slumped in the back of a pub.
In 1988 three masked men cut the telephone wires and blew electric fuses of the power lines to a Glasgow housing estate. At this point, he assured me, the trio did not need to do any more

for the numerous residents living there were already starting to panic in fear with the neighborhood isolated for some unknown sinister purpose. They did continue onto a certain policeman's house where they, 'Opened his front door with a chainsaw'. All the small details, as to what they did that night, assured me he was one of them responsible. When he finished telling this story, he asked "Do you have a chainsaw?"
"Yes, I've got a nice Husqvarna in the shed." I replied.'

Life is a funny old game. We can always remember where we are when we first heard a certain famous person has died. Two I remember most vividly were Elvis and Princess Diana - a strange couple you might say. There I was with a pile of calf shit measuring up to my lower chest as a eight-year-old attempting to shovel it with the farmer's stout son when he appeared to announce Elvis was dead. At the time it didn't make much difference to me because that pile still looked like a mountain towering before me in tandem with an interest in Presley that wasn't great. Concerning Princess Diana; upon hearing about her death I'd came down the stairs in the early afternoon after another drunken Saturday night to hear the shocking news. There were pictures on television therefore I knew this was a day to remember. Not that I had any particular fondness for the British Royal Family, likewise, such sentiments were shared for they had little fondness for her. Royals were staying in the Scottish Highlands at Balmoral Castle. Word filtering out from inside the building was just as the public seen it; they had little or no remorse for the lady and were forced into a public display of sympathy later on that day due to a simmering public outcry just to preserve their popularity.

We all remember September the Eleventh 2001. Where we were, what we were doing at the time when hearing the news. I was helping a brother when he shouted down the stairs from his workshop, as I was working outside, that an airplane just hit the World Trade Center. When he soon heard after on the radio a second plane hit the second tower, I shouted back up to him this must be a joke, with the advice, 'Don't believe it'. Without the benefit of television pictures to guide my judgment, I couldn't be more wrong. I was probably one of the last people to see the catastrophic event on television because we worked late that night, then I talked for hours outside the house with a friend before finally viewing what would be once in a lifetime pictures. People will always remember those pictures of both airplanes making direct hits on the Twin Towers, but having taken so long to see them they already had Osama Bin Laden as part of the spiel. Bin Laden, rightly or wrongly, was pronounced guilty in the eyes of the world due to such portrayal. Two other airplanes were featured in what I saw as one being downed in the countryside and another at the Pentagon with a security guard keeping television crews at a distance if like they had something to hide on the matter?! At the time it looked like the Pentagon had not suffered an airplane impact but an explosion from a bomb such were the meager details emerging in footage. Once you have experienced most of life's drastic situations it becomes instinctive to what the scenario really is. I could be said to have lived that life, therefore this left an eerie feeling about the Pentagon...

Time passed, where I only ever had a passing interest in the World Trade Center incidents being so cynical about how the Western World is behaving. This was until I heard the allegation, 'The Israelis are blackmailing the Americans over the September the Eleventh attacks.'

What?

Initially I left this one to go over my head, but, if you like conspiracies, this has to be the ultimate in modern times. Meanwhile, in France a book was published that became a best-seller alleging no airplane hit the Pentagon building. This book detailed out a strong argument in favor of what it claimed. A case was growing to expose or dispel a massive conspiracy. The likes of which could rank alongside Rosswell and John F Kennedy's assassination. On the internet there are various web sites with spy photographs showing the Pentagon after the supposed crash. These pictures show no wreckage from the airplane that supposedly hit the building, no evidence of aviation fuel (kerosene) having caused the explosion, no evidence of fuel burning in the surrounding areas (fuel as a liquid only burns off the vapor on top of it where it will flood the surrounding area when alight), a ground based large hole in a wall when it was meant to be an airborne craft that caused it, and an area of contact with the Pentagon wall looking like it was too small for the size of airplane they were claiming smashed through it!

After a light aircraft crashed locally, I was told you could find curled up pieces of aluminum foil, once unrolled these could contain a little human flesh of deceased aviators. No such intimate telltale grizzly details were mysteriously ever told about the Pentagon incident.

All along I had an uneasy gut feeling about this forth attack ever since I seen a security guard keeping the media at bay. The World Trade Center attacks are undeniable - yet Building 7 behind them fell down for no reason as a *BBC* reporter read out it was going to predicting the event as it happened?! - but the Pentagon was attacked at ground level suggesting explosives were brought in by a road going vehicle then detonated, and not the impact of an air borne craft that would have to nosedive severely. Terrorist pilots of those planes were allegedly reported to have only sought training on how to maintain level flight yet the crash here was of a landing maneuver; if that's what happened? Alternatively, the explosion was more in keeping with a missile being fired at it!

If the truth was being stifled, who was really responsible? When I seen the television late at night on September the Eleventh, Osama Bin Laden was already pronounced guilty by media association, but this did not correspond with the later said Israeli allegation nor did it correspond with a potential internal attack on the Pentagon. Israel and the terrorist network Al-Qaeda are sworn enemies, but to complicate what was seen there were ordinary Palestinians celebrating the success of the attacks. This footage was quickly erased from later news reports. Most likely because it could be found too offensive due to the high mortality rate. Allegations also exist that the Palestinians were not the only ones celebrating these atrocities, where a group of Middle Eastern men were arrested at a viewpoint overlooking New York at the relevant time. These men were alleged to be a jubilant group of Israelis, camcorders in hand, positioned to film the attacks! Conflicting views were materializing from different sources. So who were those that knew in advance? And, why did they know? Is the United States open to blackmail on the subject; and if so, why?

I always look for the obvious. Like if American Intelligence or the Government planned assisted or knew in advance about the attacks in any way, and if Israelis knew the truth or conspired in it, hence the blackmailing allegation; is there any evidence to support this? How much did they really know? Was it, for example, that they let it happen? Conspiracy theorists choose the let it happen allegation as a means of drawing the United States into the Second World War by means of the Japanese attack upon Pearl Harbor. They also go by did it happen allegation from attacks on US warship Maddox in the Gulf of Tonkin, which started American involvement in the disastrous Vietnam War. Both insinuations have been applied to September the Eleventh.

After September the Eleventh the Israeli Government demanded a massive aid package from the United States. In the history of present day Israel, American dollars has always financed this nation, but the difference here is they did not appear to be asking or begging, more like extorting massive amounts of wealth. There was also the case of Israel firing a missile into neighboring Syria at what they claimed was a terrorist camp, where, instead of George W Bush condemning such in accordance with international law, he praised Israel for her bold action - although there is a pattern of such practices. Or, continued support at the United Nations council for Israel from the United States against what would appear to be the face of reason. Other niggling incidents such as Israelis being arrested and expelled from the States have been apparent since the attacks. The percentage of Jews who died in the World Trade Center was incredibly low compared to the number who should have been present. Finally; why did the two nationalities have frosty relations after?

What may be connected to all this was the fact the Israelis evacuated their embassy in the States after the planes hit! Who were they running scared from? When you consider the Bin Laden family (some of whom are half-brothers to Osama) were escorted out of America with State protection at a time when Osama was the chief suspect yet Israelis mysteriously chose to flee without the specialized protection and authority of US Government agencies. Osama Bin Laden has remained the only suspect for these crimes, if the American Intelligence is to be believed. The hypocrisy to all of this is astounding suggesting we have never been told the full truth.

If there is any truth to these allegations; where did it all begin? Does anybody consider Monica Lewinsky being part of a larger conspiracy? Was she the unintentional seed that grew into the catastrophe that shook the world? Was President Bill Clinton intentionally removed from Office to make way for George Bush Junior, as someone of low IQ and questionable moral character that would oblige the conspirators in the execution of this plan? Since the attacks, the United States has been plagued with Bush did it allegations. When Bill Clinton denied ever having 'sexual relations with that woman' the Secret Service and others would have been well aware of his philandering, if not with Lewinsky then possibly with other women and young girls. From that very public denial it was possible to remove a sitting President. I was suspicious of this scenario when you consider other cases of leading officials around the world having evidence against them disappear - in England former Prime Minister Ted Heath was alleged to be sodomizing young boys, where afterward they were allegedly murdered to prevent witnesses materializing although the British Secret Service were said to be fully aware of such antics?! Likewise, with other world leaders, suspects have been known to disappear. Why was there no such assistance given to Clinton? Has the corrupt world we live in finally cleaned up its act, or has it gotten a lot worst? Another variation on this is to consider the murder of John F Kennedy where the supposed bullet that killed him appeared beside his corpse though it did not resemble the mangled projectile it should have been, or, as a single object, capable of inflicting multiple wounds. Bill Clinton is the first American President to be impeached in over a century – just consider all the scandals that have gone down in that period never indicting the sitting President then it does make his removal questionable.

The 2000 election had Al Gore win the most votes. In a democracy this should have elected him President, but due to ballot rigging allegations in the State of Florida the presidency went against him. Powerful people would appear to be influencing Bush's win. His father was said to have been director of the CIA before he took Office. Was assistance given from this quarter to assist his stupid son? Was there reason to continue a family dynasty other than a historic father/son first?

For these reasons my skepticism increased about who was behind the most spectacular terrorist attack committed in recent history. For I have never believed one man supposedly hiding in a cave in remote Afghanistan could mastermind and pull off such a stunt, where in the process eluding American Intelligence with all its many allies. Days after the attacks, the editor of *Globe* magazine was poisoned with Anthrax where this publication previously issued wanted pictures of Osama Bin Laden. Pundits were always going to connect the two incidents (maybe too conveniently) to be left thinking a faction of Al-Qaeda murdered the editor thereby reinforcing perceived guilt of Bin Laden. Anthrax was posted from within the States, which is curious to think a terror network of this nature possesses elements used in biological warfare internally. Why didn't they use such chemical agents to wipe out an entire city by putting them in the water supply?

The worst cases of Anthrax killing people in recent times is in the city of Glasgow, where it has several times been included in the heroin supplied on the streets to junkies.

Finally, once I was left questioning all this, at the 9/11 commission set up to establish the truth a leading military general said three planes were involved then quickly corrected himself in the same sentence to say four. He should know the truth. So why couldn't he count to a number less than the fingers on one hand? I was already skeptical before his omission got broadcast...

If not considering September the Eleventh the greatest act of terrorism, then, what was?

A homegrown attack was what I considered the worst; this being Lockerbie. It is a small Scottish village not far up the M74 motorway from England that suffered the most catastrophic act of terrorism in Europe. An airplane crashed there in 1988 when a bomb exploded inside the craft to send wreckage scattering down upon the village. That night all on-board perished plus locals on the ground. In total this terrorist act claimed two-hundred and seventy lives. The incident remains the worst in Europe. At the time it was referred to locally as, 'The poppy fields of Lockerbie', due to the amount of heroin allegedly scattered over the countryside from the crash site. A fact the authorities denied, and, likewise, this fact was absent from the court-case that convicted a Libyan. Although initial focus centered upon Iran in a revenge attack for downing two of their airliners by the American Navy, suspiciously this was suddenly dropped. It took about twenty years for the authorities to finally admit CIA agents were on-board this flight. Such an admission corresponded with what was originally said; it was alleged locally (and internationally) this was a CIA drugs run that all went wrong. An alleged corresponding story being; Iran sought revenge for the downing of their airplanes so sponsored a Palestinian group called the PFLP-HQ to act on their behalf when not wanting to be directly involved in what could result in war between Iran and the US. These Arab terrorists knew the CIA were importing heroin so substituted a case for one with a bomb in it - it is often alleged such was never searched at customs because their baggage got diplomatic immunity?! The airplane then got delayed in Germany, which meant instead of exploding over the Atlantic Ocean making it difficult to conduct an investigation it blew up over Scotland scattering evidence down upon the countryside around Lockerbie. Piece by piece, evidence and differing sources supported this view yet a presumably innocent Libyan was convicted when a crucial Maltese witness, upon receiving a massive pay-off to provide evidence that went in opposition to the convicted man's circumstances, testified against him?!

All of which occurred involving high level players with fabrication and manipulation, or otherwise...

The sixty-four thousand dollar question being; what was the greatest act I ever committed upon being rated the most dangerous man in Britain?

All along I didn't want this title nor could I live up to perceived expectations. I felt it an albatross around my neck. However, there is a saying; be careful what you wish for! Not what I wanted but what the authorities were hoping for to justify their policy of mass murder (or genocide as stated by a UN human rights representative) with a targeted individual they could proportion some blame onto, or use to justify their dastardly actions and injustices – was I being manipulated for this purpose? I don't know, but there remains that distinct possibility... However, the cart obviously came before the horse for I DID LIVE UP TO THIS STATUS BUT IT TOOK ELEVEN YEARS TO GET THERE?! In GCHQ or MI5 headquarters, they must have been looking into a crystal ball to know who was going to fulfill this role so long into the future...

Upon living quietly in the Republic of Ireland until the year of change of 2004 for this was when the SAS were once again dispatched after me in earnest. Initially, a Welshman appeared looking somewhat out of place being in such superb powerful athletic condition but appeared to do nothing, just hanging around idly drinking in local pubs living alone in the same small west Irish village. He went by the name Martin Jones, claiming to be a cousin to Welsh European boxing champion Colin Jones. Facial likenesses being of such close family familiarity there was obviously an element of truth to this, plus the age bracket could be considered appropriate. SAS never operate alone (in military operations they are said to operate in groups of four each with an unique area of expertise, but they have been short-staffed in recent times so this doesn't always follow), so when a colleague to pair up with was drafted into a neighboring village it all became apparent – the death squad were in position to kill another innocent Scot, as per. Awkwardly, undisguised when the second member arrived in a blue jeep, standing at over six foot tall wearing baggy clothes to hide his physic, he would curiously creep around the side of it if pretending to be invisible when entering or exiting, but in fact stood out blatantly due to these strange quirks (materializing from how to avoid surveillance). With all military personnel they become too regimented to display bizarre social traits that are easy to pick out if you have an eye for it. Likewise, their fashion sense can be ten years out of date, probably from never updating from when they first enlist and being usually surrounded by men most of the time. This circumspect tall stranger was David Gilles, originally from the north of England.

Once in position the attacks would begin. When matters warmed up this went go on to include a dubious pair parked up in the local street in a beat-up old red *Volkswagen* (*Passat* perhaps?) car sitting there padded out in what would be *Kevlar* under flak-jackets. Presumably, they were Irish Rangers (an armed paramilitary defense force positioned between police and army utilized to deal with the most dangerous in Ireland). I often reminisce about those days recalling how I was the only side in this awkward triangle unarmed, and, the fact the SAS could operate freely when fully under Irish surveillance?! In the end I took off to France, where on return to die fighting this British Army pair (plus take the odd stray bullet from Irish Rangers) there was found no need to because Jones got himself flung out the regiment. His departure was featured in *The Sun* (October 2004) tabloid newspaper, but written disguising the fact when saying it was due to him fighting with his girlfriend - if that were true the SAS would have no members whatsoever. So I survived with Martin Jones in the aftermath now stringing himself up unable to live with what he'd become when no longer being part of the British death squads, thereby having to face life from the outside alone with the haunting consequences of the monster they reduced him to.

Such should be a warning to all those who dream about joining what is in essence a scumbag regiment - there you have the truth, accept it or reject it?!

Shortly after, the local battalion of Provisional IRA members would also be instrumental in ultimately saving his life when they threatened him. This was paramount to restoring fighting spirit thereby giving him the will to live again. Otherwise, when his girlfriend kicked the front door in when he was strung up. Such was a genuine incident on examination of the marks in the wooden panels with her being local Irish therefore not parley to any conspiracy. Gilles, in these times, lay low in the other smaller village.

2006 began with forewarning to what was coming down the pipeline when the Government of George Bush Jr announced in conjunction with alleged war-criminal Tony Blair they were to crack down on their enemies – that being who *they* judged to be terrorists, dissidents, etc. Basically, anybody they took a dislike to, whence Scotland was suffering a claimed genocide solely because they could kill there with impunity! Such were bleak prospects for all Scots... This, in my eye, seemed to possess foundation for there was the case of SNLA member, MacIntosh, with him a close likeness to me, being suspiciously found dead in a Scottish prison cell shortly after the clampdown was announced. His status was then artificially glorified upon death with tabloid reports saying he was a terrorist leader. SNLA were such a small grouping where I knew who the actual leader was (then living in Ireland) and who the supervisor in the Cumnock workshop feared most. Neither of whom went by this surname.

With Martin Jones no longer solely positioned in the vicinity to kill. He, however, continued to live on in the company of the lady who saved his life, where he would often smile or slyly wink just to subliminally say something like, 'I know who you are and you know who I am, yet you never once went squealing to the police and would have died in combat'. Sometimes I acknowledged these discreet actions with a complementary smile for they were respectful in a circuitous manner given he now recognized what the British State had done to him. His girlfriend must have been bemused if she noticed such clandestine communications.

With British State agents never about to operate in a decent upstanding manner new recruits were drafted in two years later (2006) to include their so called legend, Bob Hope look-a-like, Sgt Tom Kennedy. Now they were sacrificing all! The big guns were here with a vengeance. This upgraded death squad possessed members to match those sighted at the scene when Jill Dando was murdered?! There was the man with trilby hat... a Mediterranean looking gentleman... others of matching descriptions... and, curiously a Bob Hope lookalike for a possible assassin (before media reports changed that to Bob Mills and had the inquiry refocus away from him/them onto a decoy bearing similarities to her fiancée)...

Sgt Tom 'Bob Hope' Kennedy appeared, from memory, on the 19th of June 2006 at the front door of my basement apartment with hair cut along the length of the neckline, this being a haircut straight out of a 1990s disco, one that quickly went out of fashion, and what he may have sported ever since the murder of Jill Dando. He claimed to live in the same building but with a problem with the post hence this face-to-face. An absentee landlady meant an appointed tenant dealt with domestic matters, including mail, where he previously told of all arrangements and described the tenants within the building. None of whom resembled Bob Hope in any shape or form. Bob Hope the impersonator was obviously lying! He was a phantom tenant with a phantom excuse from a phantom world, but with sinister intentions. I worked it out when the words left his mouth, with them beginning in a fake Irish accent but unable to maintain this forgery thereby finishing off in a more genuine softer south English tone. A face-to-face is their way of checking it is the right person and surveying the overall environment before returning for the execution. This I am a hundred percent certain of. Thought patterns at the time combined with past experiences said there would be a one day delay followed by the kill… Without taking into account urgency on the matter with my rising status (could it go any higher?) it was rather surprising when they returned early, next day, with David Gilles and others in what were a full death squad kitted out for the main event!

I was walking alone up the sloping street towards the apartment, but on the pavement on the opposite side from, when a packed blue jeep (Gilles') slowed down for further facial recognition – all occupants eyeballing me - then departed at haste to go nose-in up to the metal railing gates leading down to the apartment. The driving was erratic. This space is always kept clear for the purpose of vehicles parking behind the blocks of flats. I diverted up to the art gallery overlooking the scene now sweating somewhat. There after I waited it out just to survive. With my refusal to come down to the gates they finally departed. I had out-flanked them again...

The next day the death squad returned for a second attempt. It was less eventful but just as precarious. Martin Jones' replacement was obviously never SAS. This I knew having previously seen him in the pub in company of a relaxed looking

Gilles who wore a distinctive pink shirt and loose fitting jeans, female colleague who always dressed in blue, and Special Branch Officer with long dreadlocks known to drive a car with the offensive and illegal letters *'FTP'* (f*** the Pope) in the registration plates. Furthermore, illegally driving without tax or insurance discs in the windscreen yet never apprehended in the Republic of Ireland?! A vehicle referred to from the inside as a Q-car. I held serious grievances-cum-doubts about Martin Jones' replacement. When first sighting him I thought he was just a little coward acting up trying to appear hard in the company of others. Remove them and he would most likely shit himself. So when escaping the present hit unarmed in a *Skoda* car I unexpectedly came face-to-face with him when driving straight up to his car's side window like I was about to T-bone it, with him sitting in the driver's seat. He would obviously be nursing a 9mm handgun (an SAS weapon of choice with him now being considered one of the group) in a holster or on his lap or concealed elsewhere in the car for quick access, but being alone with the other personnel separated and distant on the street below he alone had to waste me here! For an SAS member such would be ideal quiet settings... Did he really have the bottle for it? A look of absolute terror on his face said not. It verified everything I knew about this low-life regime and the plastic hard-cases they have when wasting tax-payers' money on such antics, yet they pin medals on *heroes* like him?!

21st June 2006 was the longest day, especially here, for from then onwards I spent four and a half months on the run.

2004 had been tough when up against an initial death squad: 2006 horrendous when an up-rated group appeared followed with the said four and a half months running. A final month of which solely due to paranoia, for there were two death squads in pursuit with what would most likely be a policy of kill-on-sight. So when 2008 rolled around this required clever thinking: 2004 produced a lucky escape with Jones and company (plus a battalion of the local Provision IRA members assisting in preserving his life to my frustration); 2006 a situation few, if any, could survive, where simple patterning upon consideration said 4 – 6 – 8 indicating death in 2008! I resigned myself to the fact it was all over... Undoubtedly I would die when renewed attempts were made in this forthcoming year. How far and for how long could anybody out-run them with their limitless resources? I was broke, getting older and slower yet I could never go through with political asylum for it irked me badly. With which, this reinforced the decision just to die fighting them. Though, this time, with a twist or two thrown in for good measure probably due to utter defiance in the absence of any realistic incentive...

At the beginning of the year it actually felt so low to be asking; what is their weakest front? Then running down options: - Police? Politicians? Military? Intelligence? Financial? Alternatively; a favored individual from within the British Establishment would be appropriate? A second alternative being, somebody implicated who'd never got his comeuppance due to what they'd done to me, my family or others? Those fitting this predicament could be drawn from a substantial expanding list! Of the considered targets, I had secured substantial victories against each target group at this point thereby bolstering confidence...

There was unbridled acknowledgement I was slowly being reduced to their level, yet they swim around in the gutter like sleazy worms permanently without issue! Now I was mulling over all possibilities and opaque interests with the intention of attacking that front, whichever one it happened to be?

The answer this exercise produced was astounding, albeit deduced from some inside information disclosing: - Afghanistan, a war of attrition (like all wars) for the SAS to be quickly followed by a return to Iraq. Although not found in mainstream media Iraq was said to be more than just a war of attrition. In simple tactical terms for Allied forces, it was a rerun of the similar Kuwait War of 1990, which ventured across into Iraq. What you didn't read in the newspapers at the time is all those early casualties of British soldiers from the next incursion into Iraq were in fact of SAS members, numerously so. For they go in first to disrupt infrastructure assassinate and sabotage equipment preparing the ground for the main body of the armed forces to advance into. Moreover, it was a lot more damning than that for the British Army because the Iraqis remembered how Allied forces operated against them in the first Gulf War only eleven years previous. Rumor-mill said Allied forces wanted the SAS to lead this new assault by preparing enemy ground first off... What are predominantly upper-class officers within the British Army in control of military procedures did not possess the foresight to change the modus operandi. From their perspective, it won the original conflict so why change a winning formula?! In short, the Iraqis knew fine well what was coming so decimated the front-line on arrival – you get the drift – who all happened to be SAS members. Such are the actions of the hooray-Henry types that control the lives of others. So I thought long and hard about this. The weakest front was therefore military. Not police nor intelligence nor political nor financial nor some obnoxious prick needing a good doing (of which there were many). It was in fact the (not-so-glorious) SAS! Crazed yet bewildered at what was being contemplated knowing the light-bulb had really gone off on this one (the fuse-box probably just blew off the wall with such a thought!), would I after eleven years of running, only periodically standing up to this evil, finally live up to the status bestowed of being Britain's most dangerous man? For I contemplated, then planned upon, wiping out an entire battalion of SAS members by whatever means possible...

Of all the escapades embarked upon, this one was always going to have its own chapter in history no matter what transpired...

Martin Jones instilled necessary confidence when acknowledging these Special Forces members were not the untouchables as portrayed, but, like everybody, each of them has an Achilles Heel! The spell was broken never to repair. I just needed to find their weaknesses to attack. So there it was, combined with a frame of mind that said: Give me the ammo and I'll go and do it: I was about to surprise the world...

With the objective set, where could I get the necessary tools for such a crazy endeavor? Was there anybody deranged or aggrieved enough as supply? When attempting to source weapons it was best to keep quiet about the overall intention for it was so outrageous, plus I needed an element of surprise to have a realistic chance of pulling this off, but it was expedient to give general hints regarding what was required hoping someone would take the bait?! The IRA, in my opinion going by past experiences, were worst than a sick joke always hovering there like flies over a rotten corpse waiting to suck its blood dry but capable of little else. Plus, whatever hardware they possess they wouldn't part with anyway. Combine that with the possibility of being ratted on if I was to engage with them and it instantly becomes a no-brainer. Gangsters (them deranged enough as supply) I knew in the past remained there. Having previously asked about breaking into a local army base I was assured all the firing pins were removed from the weapons they train with there. There were no weapons available. Bleak prospects were mounting... Not to be outdone I would revert to fighting with bloodless tactics once again. Information would be the only weapon so it had if utilized best it could. In relation to which, Denis Donaldson was a member of *Sinn Fein* and a British informer, where like nearly all such people he was found murdered once no longer employed by the security forces. I had more than an inclination regarding who was responsible…

So the target group was chosen from simple deduction. With it, I would exert another of my crazy principles, that being to take them out from the top down. In this occasion, to look for the greatest threat and then attack him first. Although 'legend' Sgt Tom Kennedy was conveniently stationed much closer plus holding the reputation (such a rep is only adhered to with his boys inside the SAS) I could see he was now little more than a half-crippled has-been, plus he would get scared when I was within striking distance – you read that correctly. I'd seen him getting nervous a few times. For all the heroic status bestowed upon him, glorification, medals, presumed to be the best they possessed, a leader of men, etc, in reality he was nothing more than a pathetic low-life and a sniffling coward! However, SAS member David Gilles was and remained the greatest threat. He did possess a danger factor. I'd seen him gun-in-hand about to murder me! Fact being, I never forgot nor forgave him for it! As for that stupid little shit-bag they used to replace Martin Jones, he was so farcical not even worth considering as a target therefore not within the criteria and probably constantly needed his nappy changing ever since the last encounter, yet he never even got what is coming to him?!

 After biding my time the moment came to tackle Gilles. Timing coincided with another incident broadcast in the media when I believed I was being targeted again, therefore it fitted perfectly by default. So I took off into the night on a bicycle armed only with an engineers' automatic center-punch, pocket-knife, spray-paint can and means of fire lighting. It was wet with drizzle hanging low. When careering down a hill blind on route to Kiltyclogher, Leitrim I hit a badger. The animal yelped in agony to recoil with which. Brakes were applied where on slowly grinding to a halt, due to dampness acting as a lubricant; I turned around to look back in sympathy at the injured beast unable to leave the tar macadam with a picture of its black and white face frozen in my mind. Black and white, good and evil, the world has never known such evil like what the British authorities inflicted upon it, such as concentration camps in South Africa, castrating Mau Mau freedom fighters in Kenya, putting death squads onto the streets of Glasgow, etc, without ever delving into the Irish situation for examples. Hesitation resided with thought but additional thinking said I had unjustly suffered enough, too much, where payback time was now... I was committed at this point so into hell I would descend never to return...

 Fire-lighting, part of the overall plan, remained in doubt due to the soaking wet environment therefore I had little means left to confront what was an intelligence cliché. For, among others, the Special Branch officer with dreadlocks also lived here.
 With deduction attained from previous reconnaissance visits I went up to the side wall of the house I believed Gilles lived to start writing in large block capitals along the wall '*KILLER LIVES HERE*' then above it standing on tip-toes to form a full sentence I wrote '*DENIS DONALDSONS*' so if interrupted when writing the graffiti the basic message was displayed first. There were no surveillance cameras to be seen, so I should not be disturbed if quiet enough about it...
 Without incident, I cycled away having decided against any fire starting to bring them out to party... Although some sort of

confrontation was expected/predicted nothing stirred upon departure. Basically, part two of this plan remained unfulfilled.

The deed was done albeit a little unsatisfactory having only partial accomplished what was intended. Time passed, with the propaganda machine eventually being rolled out giving a fanciful story of IRA dissidents from South Armagh (an IRA stronghold) crossing the entire country to murder Denis Donaldson in remote Donegal. Few Irish believed this when suspecting involvement from Crown forces. For it entailed a standard method of first leaking his address publicly in the press before the hit-squad arrived (this is allegedly done to reduce suspicion of their involvement). Furthermore, he was previously given a genuine guarantee his life was not in danger from Republicans. Donaldson was killed in early summer of 2006, where these events described were now in the summer of 2008. When after, increased surveillance on me occurred in October 2008. Correspondingly, I received wind of SAS member/s being executed by their own?! The bush telegraph machine was in over-drive; but, who was murdered and where?

Inside an Irish *Credit Union* one of the Provisional IRA escapees from the Maze Prison was asking in a derisory manner if the (British) Secret Service were still actively in pursuit. I confirmed they were. Further relaying inside knowledge about an SAS member/s being executed, hinting I was somehow involved in ongoing events. He was told to check this out, in particular to look at the small print – that being to read between the lines and work out what really happened and not what in duplicity is falsely stated on the surface. The only thing was there was no mainstream media reports to look at. Finally, on the Saturday morning, two full days later, reports started emerging of the SAS being in disarray. Leader, Sebastian Morley, led his men off the field in Afghanistan leaving Allied forces vulnerable to attack. Taliban fighters upon seizing the opportunity surprised a military storage depot to drive off in *Hummers* jeeps loaded up with untold amounts of Western armaments. They also surged upon what had been the safe haven of Kabul to deliver a consecutive defeat. These events were a turning point in the war orchestrated by myself thousands of miles away, yet few ever worked out how or what I did or accept I'd been the instigator. That particular IRA man would be in no doubt for I previously told him I'd removed the head of MI5, when at that time commenting, 'Who else could?'[Details of which are at the end of this chapter]! For me the double whammy was complete.

Sebastian Morley went on to damningly repeatedly slate the British Government stating they had 'blood on their hands!', though never fully elaborating. This corresponded with what I was claiming. *Wikileaks* published corresponding evidence to support my version of events. It came in agreement from all sides supporting the fact the official version of events was false, as is common practice with them involved in these matters, whereas what I originally claimed (before becoming increasingly shy on the matter) was standing up to scrutiny!

When I went after David Gilles it was naively a test of democracy to see if he and a colleague would stand trial for the murder of Denis Donaldson and, if convicted, get locked up for it, but such a scenario could implicate Government Ministers. So, he obviously became a pawn in this game of Russian roulette. In this instance the ramifications became monstrous. Here we had a situation running out of control. I also back-tracked believing I'd gone too far, but it was too late for the truth was out. Word for word what I claimed was proving accurate to the letter where the official version looked ropey at best, where the implications ran and ran...

Regarding me wanting to wipe out an entire battalion of SAS members, well it could be argued I did. I appear to be the most genuine character, even if it is done by default?! Afterwards the regiment went on a recruitment drive – the first time ever they were known to publicly do so for they choose members from within the armed forces when given full ongoing assessment of and don't advertise for candidates – but obviously Morley wasn't the only member not to return to active duties…

The Jackal had sprung…

In reference to the above mentioned incident:
During a conversation with an employee of the *BBC* it was agreed I should give them a copy of my book *Who Killed Jill Dando*. She, in her prime, was the golden girl of the corporation. Within hours of making that telephone call the head of MI5, Eliza Manningham-Buller, resigned saying her employment contract was for four and a half years. This was an unusual length of term, if genuine?! Alternatively, her resignation then was to mitigate against, or not wishing to answer to, MI5's involvement in the murder of Dando?! Respected journalist Richard Hall makes a compelling argument her murder was a State affair – what they term executive action – and shows in a video an uneasy Tony Blair talking on it with an inescapable depiction of guilt all over his face?! At this time I'd already been visited by SAS Sgt Tom Kennedy, a so called legend for such acts, who was of perfect match to the description given out about her killer before details got obscured. Likewise, his MI5 back-up team in Ireland fitted the descriptions of those seen near her house.

To meet my obligation I had to retrieve a copy of the book (in CD form). A first stop proved fruitless when found vacant, which meant racing the car into the night to cover 200 miles to a second repository where a CD copy was obtained. Upon knowing this call had put me on the front-line once again I kept the hammer down speeding down back-roads until '*BOOM!*' the car exploded! Full lock to full lock the steering got ratcheted to no avail. Over a half broken hedge and fence the car landed upside-down in the middle of a field with its lights on. I was barely conscience. Strung upside-down in the wreckage I needed to recover some facilities with an interior filled with smoke and cordite irritating eyes and throat. It becomes surreal. In the third person I was asking myself, "Are you still alive?"

Pain and feelings said this remained a mortal existence.

"Are you paralyzed?"

A wiggle of the head then a hand down between my legs to crunch my testicles said yes.

"How many limbs do you have?"

A quick slap of all four indicated they were all attached. Special Forces survival techniques were kicking in, in particular, about squeezing the balls! Not knowing what really happened but aware of multiple explosions the situation remained precarious as I struggled to free myself to slither out of the side-window into mud. It would appear I was not the only one curious as to the cause and my wellbeing?! Irish police officers came into the house I was registered to – although not living there then due to security precautions – asking for somebody by anther distinctive Scottish name; they were obviously looking for me but in a deceptive manner. In the resulting furor at least six agencies were trying to track me down from Irish Social Services to MI5. Why did they bother? As I sat alone in the back of the pub lifting beers with my left hand, for the right arm was paralyzed, plus attempting to conceal the right side of my head under a mop of hair. It was swollen flat with the ear. From all those in pursuit I never hid, ran nor answered too. Later on it went quiet. Somebody, unknown, obviously called the dogs off. To conclude the episode, it was the head of MI5 who provided ultimate validation my story was accurate. Her resignation date was found to be false. She had only been employed four years and three months?! Later, they attempted to disguise the fact but this discrepancy remains prominent. From which, this could imply MI5 did have Jill Dando murdered, where the reason behind it was their policy of mass murder that I had temporary disrupted. However, all the pieces remain in place for a full scale slaughter at a moment's notice, so they were never concerned about what they did only trying to cover it up or protect themselves from future prosecution…

'How can I be hung for treason when this land is foreign to me?'

6. QUESTIONABLE MOTIVES.

'At the party that night, when a girl started saying she had been the victim of a kidnapping I did not believe her. Truth is, very few people ever get kidnapped, and when they do it becomes front-page news. I just thought she was trying to impress me, boy meet girl, that sort of thing. So in an effort to keep the conversation going I gave an enthusiastic, "That's interesting."
"It is, Chubby," she replied.
"You were driving the car that done it to me."
I was certain about this one, that it definitely wasn't me, therefore protested with, "No, you've got the wrong person."
She went on to explain in minute detail certain features about myself and car to convince me her story was genuine. My disbelief abated with the thought that an incident had occurred, but she had not been kidnapped but abducted. She was young, she'd misconstrued the facts, but what became certain was she

remained grateful that I had been the driver that day for I'd rescued her from the predicament.'

As I sat there on the step watching a four-year-old run the streets, wild and carefree. The little boy shared the same round face, brown eyes and light colored hair. A comparison didn't stop there, for he had a broken arch in one of his ears. I sat there wondering; would he play the same tricks I did before him? Such as when going to the barber's shop I would wind up the man snipping because I also had a broken arch in an ear to make the head's profile look isometric once shorn. When the hair-cutter has finished and the mirror is produced to look at the back and sides of your head, it is then he asks, "Is that okay?"

It is a curious thought; why should anyone want to see the back of their head? Anyway, I would squint into the large mirror in front to allow observation of the second, just to pretend I was interested and then say sternly, "No; take a bit more off the sides; especially the left side."

The barber would be caught out every time when the next thing felt were the scissors rapidly cutting through the left amid protests of, 'Both sides are even'. A grown man having to cut other people's hair for a living just had to be wound-up in my estimation. Would this little kid grow up to be as devious? Would he come home from the barber's shop laughing but sporting unusual haircuts, leaving his mother thinking he was the worst barber in the country?

On a more serious note; watching that kid play made me wonder, when he is old enough would he hear associated stories where out of curiosity ask, "What did you really do?"

If he ever did pose such a question the only answer, due to how I suffered, would be, "Don't do what I did."

Then I thought about the situation some more; the only reason that little kid and every other kid on the street was safe then was because I and two others had the heart and backbone to do what needed doing irrespective of the danger. Then I thought again about the question theoretically asked one more time, where the answer was now, "When you grow up, you will be one spineless bastard if you don't do what I did."

To sit there in contradiction, I realized there is no definitive answer to this predicament. Life is after all a never ending sequence of paradoxes with one exception; child abuse is never acceptable [a lesson some members of the IRA should learn (referenced in the final chapter)].

In general it is poverty, social exclusion and ignorance that gives rise to an underclass who become terrorists. These can be people that only have each other with little to lose in a material sense. It is a strange quirk of human nature people from the most deprived areas defend them more vigorously compared with those from affluent surroundings. Wealthy people are in general favored, whereas the poor are readily wrongfully suspected of crime. Police bias is also predominating. Sometimes there are those who look for a cause to attach themselves to, to give themselves a sense of belonging, but in general it is circumstances that force people into a reaction. Human nature is such most people will go out of their way to avoid aggravation.
Oppression and injustice are the root causes of most acts of terrorism and materialize in many different shapes and forms, as I will demonstrate with this next experience.

An uncle invented spherical induction and exhaust valves to replace the poppet valves inside the cylinder head of the four-stroke internal combustion engine. His design was technically brilliant with a lot of marketing potential due to the fact this type of engine is the backbone of the automotive industry. He asked me to produce technical drawings required so he could submit them to the Government supported development agency. This I duly did.
What had the potential to be a ground breaking design never received the support it deserved – they gave him no support at all. No; after some horse trading nothing more came of this contact. Then, a couple of years later *Honda*, as one of the largest automobile companies in the world, took out a patent on the same design. At this my relation went back to the agency relaying this development to them in an inquisitive manner thinking a response would be to at least acknowledge the dilemma in hand. Their answer was to deny ever having any

contact with him! Interesting I thought, whereas my relation was livid, especially here when he held hard evidence to contradict their denial, plus myself as an additional witness. His design could no longer be dismissed as irrelevant now that a major international company patented the idea, which does pose questions about the integrity of them involved.

You could be forever guessing what really happened here. From, similar designs have a habit of appearing at roughly the same time, to, alleging they sold his idea onto *Honda*. When the plastic nylon was invented it derived its name from the two locations in which it was produced at the same time: New York and London – NY Lon. If you choose to accept my uncle's idea was given sold or reproduced from within this office to a third party, was an individual or a consortium responsible? Or, was it so far-reaching that the Secret Service lay being behind this corruption? How far did the treachery stretch? Scotland is a small community if you have the right contacts, but I never received a definite answer here, even with a vested interest in the subject.

A few years later I had the good fortune of being in conversation with someone from Dundee who told of his experience with the same Government assisted agency. What he claimed was a carbon copy of what happened to my uncle, word for word, name for name, and timescale for timescale. I could hardly believe what I was listening to. An identical coincidence with both men convinced they had been ripped-off in the same manner. He went on to claim he knew of a third person who suffered the same injustice in the same circumstances. Three separate individuals claiming a million to one coincidence no longer sounds like a coincidence - I am too cynical about British authority dominated Scottish society to accept this. Further, in light of other coincidences found not to be accidental upon closer inspection; why should I be trusting here? Multiply a million to one, by a million to one, by a million to one, and these are odds a bookmaker will calculate for a bet on this.

Later on, I was attending the New Enterprise Workshop in Ardeer making up my own design of frame when the supervisor repeatedly said I should seek assistance from the development agencies - the same people I was wary of. A long list of excuses not to do so, including the experience of this relative and two others, finally ran dry to my dismay and so to keep the supervisor sweet I was forced into approaching the agency – the lions' den. There I was hoping I could string out the process long enough so to have my project finished before the inevitable interference, in whatever shape or form, materialized. This is Scotland, when you live under a dictatorship you become very suspicious about all forms of officialdom and any Government backed agency. The higher standing the individual or the more prominent the authority the more distrust I attach to them. Further, all those awarded with medals from the Queen are particularly suspect to me?! A case and point being Jimmy Saville showing off a medal when many knew this to be a devious pervert?! My judgment regarding Saville and others is summarized by: How did they really rise to that position or obtain such recognition? Alternatively, about the rich; where did they get it from?

So a begrudged approach was finally made to the agency where, fortunately, I was given someone other than who had dealt with my uncle. So just maybe there was half a chance of not being done over altogether. Once negotiations progressed I was asked to submit a drawing with a detailed description of my design (needlessly so). The person requesting this suddenly changed from who was originally dealt with to the same person who could possibly have ripped-off my uncle and others. Now the alarm bells were ringing. All along the last thing I wanted to do was submit any unprotected data to this office, especially not to him. Never one to be beat by those types of people, of course I would *oblige*. With a mind as devious as mine I would rise to the challenge... The devil inside was wriggling like a snake in a hot sandpit. What could be payback for my uncle's experience beckoned! I thought about it, there was the supervisor from the workshop breathing down my neck on one side and the *helpful* agency on the other (that was never known to assist anybody I knew of). So I had to produce something otherwise I may be asked to leave the premises. I held no malice towards the supervisor because he was probably originally pressured by his superiors where that pressure was coming down the line to force me to go to the dreaded bureaucrats.

The pen went *astray* when producing the drawing and the worded technical description was more complex than need be so as to fool them examining the design. If they were clever, which I very much doubted (a train of thought being, if they were they wouldn't be in this position), they would see this design (or more accurately the faulty design submitted) wouldn't work. My skill against that of the pen-pusher/s with a design that could end up in Japan resulting in embarrassment for whoever was responsible if there was any ongoing treachery. This was how I seen it, rightly or wrongly so. They would meet their match here. Particularly when I never believed any assistance was forthcoming, but if it was what was given as a decoy was sufficient to receive it.

The supervisor held a keen interest in these activities, plus he remained rather proud of the stroke pulled on the development agency – with him probably skeptical too but unable to convey his true feelings. In such a position, it would be unwise to broadcast an opinion because he could lose his job if found to be bad-mouthing such related Government departments, employed as he were in a council funded workshop. This was all very well until his boss appeared. Where, with me working outside the office door I could hear the deception being re-laid to him. Originally I asked the supervisor to keep matters quiet because we were in a small community that might not appreciate such antics. There wasn't much appreciation here when the big boss started jumping up and down in anger, shouting, *"GET HIM OUT OF HERE, HE IS A FUCKING LIAR."*

I worked away quietly with the solemn thought, 'Take your insults to the three I know of who are convinced they have already been conned by this Government (backed) agency, where all you can do is encourage the situation.'

It all became irrelevant because after this incident I was thrown out of the workshop. It was lose lose, but with what I'd done it was to lose the least with a means of retaliation thrown in. Where, for certain, the supervisor was now being pressured. Incidentally, the manager was a Labour Party man. Injustices members of this Party did me never ends, knew no bounds, and then they have the cheek to call themselves socialists. That's not what I call them.

In central Scotland, in the 1980s-90s to be a member of this political party was usually a must-have qualification to being in those types of position. The community was constantly plagued with jobs-for-the-boys' allegations - ability being a secondary consideration. It is derogatory to think these people can deny the overall population so much by way of opportunities (and justice) and then insult them for it.

Now it could be said that I am paranoid, but from the beginning I was the very one keeping an open mind on this uncle's predicament, never dismissing or accepting any suggestion. Of this and other incidents, I generally try to keep an objective stance until the evidence is overwhelming. Truth is, I had three unconnected individuals all with the same identical complaint but I don't know of a single Scot to be assisted. They claim their purpose is to create enterprise and employment, where wealth from which will be fed back into society. A budget is in place, but, where are the results? I have never seen them; has anyone ever seen them? Do they exist? In this era double glazing companies appeared to be obtaining grant money but no other type of business. A double glazing company went onto sponsor both *Glasgow Rangers* and *Glasgow Celtic.* Needless to say the suspicious character for a replacement contact never assisted me either, nor did I ever receive receipt for the final (abstract) submission from him (which is most curious?!), unlike my uncle. Were they learning as they went along? Were they forewarned or taking a position where they could deny all involvement once again? After, I often wondered if my design ended up in Japan followed by a quick apology...

Skepticism was reinforced by two other events; one, a friend working in a similar position said she was fed up having to lie to people every day. Unable to cope with the deceit she ended up in a women's retreat. And two; once before I had been in the office in question whereon approach by a philosophical employee, she told me in all honesty, "You're wasting your time here, Son. It's all a kidology."

Not being naive, I agreed, "I know."

Even those inside the operation are blatantly sick of what is going on without any hint of a major fraud that may exist.

Scotland has for a long time had a failing business economy. Is it any wonder once you know how bad it really is for the native citizens? Just how much of this is due to deliberately imposed obstacles? In contrast to this, when I was in that workshop the genius of the people there could possibly be the best in the world. A majority of whom were not in regular employment. Unemployed trying to break out of the desperate circumstances only to be confronted with situations like the one described. The public are suckered into these pitfalls, usually by means of a cash incentive, reinforced by what could be deliberately imposed poverty. Whereas potentially being wise to the system didn't benefit me either, but at least I gave them nothing other than misery just to frustrate the situation. Maybe I am not such a rogue after all. Somebody needs to challenge them, give them a bloody nose, where with it a warning not everyone is a doormat. Someone has to challenge the oppression and tyranny in all aspects of Scottish life. This is how it was; where at that time it was not a country being governed for the native people. As implied, it was simply impossible to break the circle. For I tried with this attempt and many others but always failed. You can spend more time and effort fighting a corrupt system than actually progressing. After which, it is doubtful you will ever be allowed to progress. It could be argued this is their overall intention. I found myself in that boat more than a few times. Scottish money, or what pittance is returned to the country from the London Chancellor, is used to pay for all this treachery and corruption. Scots no longer fight this oppression. The poor sods emigrate instead, hence, for a while, the highest emigration rate in the Western World. Well here I am today as another example always having to live abroad in forced exile, but such were my experiences from home I found it difficult to trust officials in other countries, but having said that, it is refreshing to find out it is different elsewhere and such agencies abroad are genuinely there to assist.

Years later, a *Jaguar/Land Rover* subsidiary company copied a suspension design I produced, but this could be due to them viewing it in a patent granted of seeing the design on the internet, therefore this could just be a straightforward infringement of my intellectual property rights.

I remember the first time I was able to borrow money, abroad, standing outside the office with it in my hand thinking, 'But I was never allowed to do this in Scotland', with further thoughts of it being the richest country in Europe yet the oppression of the indigenous population is absolute. It was only once abroad did I truly acknowledge what was occurring...

There are many ways to oppress people, economically being another example. This is favored by the authorities because there is less evidence, less repercussions, less potential for concerted action to oppose it, especially if it is accomplished in combination with a clever propaganda campaign utilized to disguise the facts. Like the case above that may be perpetuating... For a long time there, native people have complained about all the best jobs and property being mostly held by English people. No coherent action can ever be put together to effectively readdress this. Without finance you have less power to confront such situations by legal methods, and legally it is questionable if it is possible to confront it, such is the prevailing situation. Any effective action therefore has to be done outside the corrupt rule of law.
On a side-note, I am not sure if I broke the law with the actions described previous, but once again they always like to hold this threat over you. This probably reinforces the view there is no law because what is there is only used against you, even as a victim.

I once read details on the internet of a group claiming to be acting as the political wing of the small SNLA terrorist group - terrorists that no longer operate at the time of reading the associated claims. On setting out their agenda, they said the aim was to conduct attacks to make Scotland economically unviable. What a joke! Oil wealth drained out the country could never account for the little inconvenience they caused. Northern Ireland is a different proposition. The island of Ireland is predominately based on limestone, which has little value as a mineral resource. From the original allegation that the British

Government retained it solely for its industrial wealth in the nineteen-twenties – Belfast was once a hub of heavy engineering such as ship building plus there was an aircraft and car manufacturer in the Province. With the decline of heavy industry and the persistent terrorist problems it became economically invalid to hold onto the territory. So why do they? The protestations of the Protestant/British/Unionist majority could be ignored and with the decline of the British Empire they relinquished many territories around the world but mysteriously retained this one. Maybe it is because they could never admit defeat having regarded Ireland as home soil for so long. A humiliation on their doorstep, that a gang of boys from the backstreets of Belfast defeated the British Army. If that was how the world seen it; how could the British arms industry be able to sell their products to other countries afterwards?

Alternatively, if Northern Ireland was free of England so might Scotland and the wealth of which no longer funding the remaining British territories.

At the time of the SNLA terrorists with a perceived struggle for independence, what was claimed to justify British governance never hit the mark. A fanciful tale emerged describing Scotland as the NATO aircraft carrier primary for American forces to use in a preemptive strike against Communist Russia, where, for this reason, this nation could never be free of British control. In reverse, it would also make Scotland the number one Russian target! An army general of questionable standing assisted in spreading this view. Now that the Cold War has long since ended, where oppression multiplied thereafter, this dispels any notion of this strategy being accurate. It would appear just to have been more propaganda.

The American Navy was based in the Holy Loch in the west of Scotland for many years. Out of which sailed nuclear submarines down the Clyde Estuary to the open waters of the Atlantic Ocean. In the end, as part of the peace dividend, the American forces tipped most of their redundant equipment into the sea and then departed. Discipline within the US armed forces cannot be the best whereon leaving it was alleged you could buy anything from the US Navy.

A promoted view of the Scottish/American military connection never held credence, but was there another reason for them to leave this part of the world other than a peace process? Once they were gone drilling platforms started appearing in the Clyde Estuary. This water is rich in oil where a nuclear submarine colliding with an oil drilling platform certainly sounds like a catastrophe most would want to avoid. Hotels were built solely for the predicted influx of oil executives. Were they waiting for the US Navy to leave before starting this exploration?

An older woman sat alone in the pub this night. Given the opportunity she introduced herself saying in a congenial manner she'd waited for a long time to meet me. For once paranoia wasn't overwhelming for it was deemed a genuine scenario. She was buying so to hold my attention. Where, as we drank together, she described an horrific episode from her past when a British Army bomb killed a few. A grotesque scene was being graphically conjured up. At this stage in life I'd done it all, been it all, seen it all, therefore never sought out such bloody past visions of death mayhem and murder for it is psychologically disturbing, but all was well here even when she described how the flesh was stripped from the bones of the dead and dying such was the impact of the bomb-blast. Thereafter she inquired how it really is. What to live the life I had lived, what I been parley to, was truly like? She was wishing me to tell it in a no-holds barred manner of the other side of the tracks; i.e. the dark side. Her beer paid the piper now I had to sound the tune... My answer truthful measured and candid, saying although I was forced to fight, where, from a young age it was inside me. I could do it. I had done it. However, it was never heroic yet there remains a paradox. No fighting should be glorified no matter how evil the opposition is, but - with this being a very large but - when out there on the front-line, so to speak, you are alive like never before. It provides an adrenaline hit most people can't comprehend. You are buzzing like nothing on Earth where such a high continues on after the event. It provides a lift for you to become superman. I began explaining how as a tiny sixteen-years-old I went out alone to die fighting off what I wrongfully thought were five grown men breaking into the house emphasizing I were so small and outnumbered. Later on in the conversation getting into details how every sense the body possesses multiplies ten-fold in such situations allowing me to do the impossible, yet repeating it is not glorious like some would have you believe. In a male only group such becomes glorified where bravado feeds bravado where them talking increase their achievements, bravery, victories, threat posed, etc... Not here, where it was a realistic reflection looking into the complexities of it all.

  I was on a local bus talking with a Glasgow friend from the seat in front, which meant I was facing backwards but with his line of vision forward in the direction we were traveling. My stop was next up. The bus was prematurely slowing down. When I looked around there was a large group of Irish travelers separated by another group facing each other over a patch of vacant ground. Furthest away group all had their backs against a line of transit vans with each man spaced out a meter or so apart with the scene reminiscent of the fictional version of *Gunfight at the OK Corral* – the historical version had very few fight, where folklore magnified the event into the distorted picture we have today.
  Turning back to face this mate, given he possessed the best view of the scenario, I asked; "Is that a set-to (confrontation)?"
He squinted more without answering. A half nod of the head indicated it might be...
I further coaxed; "Can you see any shotguns?"
His head wiggled side-to-side some more adjusting the line of vision to see what was on the street. Again, no reply?! He sat dumbfounded uncertain regarding what he/we were surveying. I never turned to look again upon trusting his judgment, which wasn't forthcoming. He was acting like my eyes and ears. Where I lived was further out past both groups, which meant passing through them all to get home... The brakes were applied slowing the bus to a halt distant from the groupings that covered the actual bus-stop. I stood up - what could have been needlessly so for I could have waited an hour for the travelers to disperse then return home - turned for what could be a last time to address my mate, to say; "It was nice knowing you."
He nodded in agreement, "It was, Rab."

Returning the compliment pleasantly to subliminally be in agreement, for we both knew this could be our parting words in this world; matter of fact they were. A fearful looking bus driver intrepidly opened the door. His white knuckles on the steering wheel said it all. Out I stepped devoid of all those who also lived there. Fearing for their lives they stayed on board. I walked up and into the first group. A lot of banter was being said. I weaved through them quietly to what should be the front-line with a surreal silence engulfing my head. Obviously an adrenaline hit was distorting perception, as per what occurs in such situations. Then like a fool I took those initial steps out into what was no-mans-land between both sides! This is the most dangerous arena because there you get blasted by buckshot from both sides. Although it doesn't kill in a human context it stings like hell. Something was amiss here?! The first group was joyful but that could just be bravado and gallows humor where nerves combined with the company of others brings it on. So with full view of the second group all facing me the fact finally struck home; they were not holding shotguns! There were no shotguns or firearms to be seen. As for group now behind me, they were predominantly women and children. What was happening here? Then I noticed it, a large bouncy castle in one of the gardens. It was a child's birthday party. Although them present had lined themselves up if readying for battle, yet, undeterred and oblivious to what could have been going down, I would have died there for no apparent reason?! It did raise questions about my frame of mind. Danger - in this case perceived danger - was no longer registering. One day in the future I would have to rejoin the human race again to live a normal life - if I could?

Questionable motives…never be fooled!

'We fought for justice and not for gain.'

7. LAWS AND RULES.

'I was once at a party where in the morning they were stuffing a body into a wheelie-bin. This was waste disposal, where I didn't know if he was alive or dead, I didn't know his name, or if he was in a coma from a drugs overdose or whatever. What became of this corpse, or otherwise, I just don't know. It is simple; you just don't ask questions, these are the rules of the game. You could torture me after but I still couldn't answer; that's how it is.'

Here was I, quiet and introverted, with a life that had descended into a *Hollywood* gangster movie where the leading actor is running from rival mobsters, running from the Feds, where there is only one law, the law of the jungle, whence you shit on no-one and in the end go down with the bullet. That's how it really is. Where the only thing you are left with is a little bit of dignity because you betray nobody and die with the bullet in the back of the head – hopefully! Most of the time you pray for the bullet in the head, but I had given myself a problem with this when the Men in Black couldn't do the job. Who was capable of wasting me if they couldn't? Was the hit-man who stalked me capable of it? Or, was he about to get the biggest surprise of his miserable life when it really came to the big showdown? For a long time I had been living solely on beer and chocolate with disregard for diet health or tooth decay. What is the point in preserving your teeth if you believe the end is near? It may look good in the coffin but later everything rots to dust. I only ask myself how it ever became this crazy. At times it couldn't get any more messed-up, such as being given an initiation service by one of the godfathers of the Provisional IRA and on the other side of the coin being given basic SAS training from an ex-member - like how to kill people with single hits. Both practices were administered on the streets of Ireland. In the end this existence no longer made any sense to me and I was supposedly living this contorted nightmare – you cannot keep living in such a manner or soon you will become detached from reality. As I found out later, one of the largest challenges would be to live a mundane existence again.

All along I had no alternative to what I did therefore bore no sense of guilt. In general, it wasn't in my nature to live this life and because of that it made me a lot more cautious compared to others full of bravado that are quickly disposed of. It is puzzling to wonder how those responsible for the oppression and terror inflicted could ever justify their actions. Can they live with themselves today? What they do to innocent people, to women and children, how they ruined an entire community and country just for a little personal gain or selfish greed. Maybe it was not for financial incentive but to impress superiors looking for promotion, recognition, or to demonstrate loyalty. All of which is certain never to be returned. Such is the fallacy they were living under for I seen firsthand with more than a few examples loyalty meant nothing to their evil masters. People living under control like that will always find some bullshit to justify their actions otherwise they can't continue. They blot out reality by finding (read pretending) a threat supposedly more sinister than what they are. Such a syndrome applies to both servant and master. Who is worse than them when they get down to a level below Adolf Hitler? Many examples could support this when demonstrating ills inflicted upon people in Scotland that Hitler never did to anybody, where it is happening to the innocent and unsuspecting.

Personal rules were simple enough; never use immediate family friends or neighbors because they are the first to be suspected of assisting. Never talk in your own house, place of work or any other regular haunt, as these buildings are likely to be bugged. For a long time it was impossible for me to have a regular job because that is so predictable where one-day I would leave the premises to be looking down a gun barrel! Preferably never do anything incriminating on regular premises. Never talk revealingly over any telephone. Fiber optic cables make tapping into a line more difficult but undercover personnel just go to the telephone exchange to do it. Mobile telephones are the best tracking and listening device you can own so you should never possess one, or, if you have a telephone, it is to leave it behind when not wanting to be tracked or listened into. Faxes and text messages are also read. The local disco was recommended by someone close to military intelligence as the best place to hold a conversation, where you have to shout into the other person's ear. No amount of detection equipment can pick up anything there. Undercover personnel may be present but limbless in this situation. In any event, would they be able to hump detection equipment into a night-club? Listening equipment is now so specialize it can be directed on an individual to solely pick out that person's words in a noisy crowd. Never use a regular vehicle for any other reason than legitimate purposes. Even then such a vehicle is likely to be tracked by manual or electronic means. The familiar television movie scene of being followed from behind with the pursuers in the rear-view mirror is not always the case. Don't use the main roads for these are now covered with security cameras. A network of (initially) blue road-side cameras was installed to cover every major route. These cameras were said to have been developed by *NASA* to provide facial recognition plus read car registration numbers night or day. Further, close-up ordinary roadside cameras are capable of discerning car registration plate numbers. E-mails are easily monitored and also provide a means of tracking people around the world because of the internet connection to the telephone network. Although the authorities like to deny they are actively pursuing this. All secure means of thwarting interference, such as firewalls, can be broken and are being broken. Within the Intelligence community, they like to avoid the use of such electronic communications for this reason. Once you change your e-mail address they can still trace you by means of who is regularly corresponded with, by certain key words unique to yourself, or, patterns of use. Just think how quickly a search engine can detect any sequence of words then you will have an idea to how quickly they can trace you. I once had an e-mail address made up in Swedish with a change in personality to avoid detection, which was not such a handicap given the old Scots language is close to Nordic dialect. When my e-mails were being hacked into, presumably by the authorities, they would open then before I did then replace them with adverts for life insurance. This is just a petty way of threatening, though I did resent the fact that not all correspondence was getting through. Or, when I caught someone casing my home in Ireland with a view to entering it when vacant, two days later the traveling salesman came around to sell life insurance once again! Any important letters have to be addressed to a secondary address so they are not opened read and resealed prior to receiving them. When this is done it is noticeable with ripples on the back of the envelope. On posting my 'Press release' to various institutions I also sent myself a copy, which took ten days to arrive. The regular postman had, at the time, been substituted by an undercover agent going by the name Kevan Smith (a most common name), who intercepted the letter then confiscated it only to realize I was behind the entire scenario hence the large delay. It is another human rights violation that the authorities confiscate your mail, but what this ploy did, in this instance, was another means of further substantiating the claims in my message were accurate. What undercover personnel like to do when following you on foot is to predict your steps, so to be in your place of business before you arrive, just like when driving when they attempt to lead the way so to reduce suspicion. When you are under suspicion you will be wary of anyone that enters a building after you. I was once set up with a honey-trap in a small lift – just me and her - with her assets bulging out of a mini dress. Of course, she had to be in there first.

A final rule (quirk) I adhered to was never to talk about current events immediately after they occur, but to let matters lie for a while then claim what I'd done. Such could be counter-productive. Where at times it looked like I was adding my name to a past event - especially so if the authorities had expertly covered it up by then leaving others to wonder what I was on about!

I have met a number of players who have mobile telephones like the latest accessory item on their person. How much easier do they want to make it for the authorities to monitor them, as they go about their business with a listening and tracking device they paid for themselves? Authorities, when monitoring them without their knowledge, must be laughing. The video phone will be an even greater asset to the spooks. There will be no mistaking who is talking in what tone or in what facial expressions, although voice recognition as a method of detection has long been a reality. Certain key words can be picked up in a general eavesdropping operating of the telephone network – mobile telephones are more suited to this kind of detection.

Now faced with all this it can be turned to your advantage like when I had an argument with a friend in the local pub when he asked, "How was Amsterdam?"

I could not make him believe I'd honestly never been in Holland before then, but he was adamant this was not the case. What had happened, so it was uncertain where I was in the world, was to have a friend post a letter home to my family from Amsterdam. The letter had been written by myself and posted from there, hence a genuine foreign postmark. I'd no reason to lie to this mate other than the fact the pub we were drinking in was a regular haunt and previously been bugged with underground cables. If my deception was convincing to him, it would surely be convincing to the spooks – then you know how successful you are! This is what I had to constantly do, that being, read the signs correctly…

With the increasing advent of technology, where new satellites are being placed in the atmosphere etcetera, the best way to avoid detection is to reject all modern advances of technology and go and sleep under a tree. Having slept in gutters all over Europe I recommend the local tennis courts for luxury - if you can find them. As the goons put greater emphasis on gadgets but reject basis techniques more so every year, this is the only way to proceed. A cozy office has less risk and better home comforts than the mountains of Afghanistan. In recent times, intelligence agencies have realized this weakness so they have reverted to putting more officers in the field.

The law in Scotland, from a personal point of view, could never be trusted where that opinion prevailed before I ever had any experience with it. Time after time all I ever needed was for the law to exist in its stated form. This legal system is accused of political bias in favor of the Labour Party, where I had never been a member or voted for them therefore knew never to see justice from such a corrupt system. How right I was. That first stunt of using the newspapers and court together to oppose the tyranny was an example of how bad it is. On the Friday beforehand, I checked the following with a capable local lawyer; if you have been victimized by police/Special Branch to the extent you have committed an offence, do you have a legitimate defense? This lawyer assured me this was the case. I now only needed the law to hold true for four days afterwards. At the trial, it was adjourned for discussions in the backroom chambers where on the barristers' return they colluded in changing the law saying my defense could only be offered in mitigation. Where did this materialize from denying me the right to a fair trial before my testimony was submitted? More importantly at the time, it denied giving extra credence to the testament for broadcasting purposes. It was guilty until found innocent just as I expected all along. Not the pretense of innocent until proven guilty like they portray to fool the gullible masses.

That one solicitor previously consulted, though I only ever knew by her first name, was the only Scottish lawyer I ever found capable of representing a client. Unfortunately, she changed practices and her former employers were evasive to where she went. Maybe they were sore at her loss.

After these exploits the next time Strathclyde Police stopped me when driving and asked I produce vehicle documents I never did, as I was still waiting for their analysis on the poisoned milk, which they never answered to. Even with the subject being brought up under oath in court it made no difference to them. In simple terms, here is a police force that do not answer to the law; so why should I? Why should anybody when the authorities commit any crime they want then never answer to it? A system as corrupt as this has to be brought to its knees by non-compliance, just like how I behave towards it. Had more people the spine to do likewise, it would soon disintegrate into the farce it really is.

My next incursion with Scottish solicitors was a sick joke to say the least. On the tenth of April 1997 my unemployment benefit was illegally terminated and after waiting months when I was originally told, 'We will take a decision on this and let you know in due course.' there never was any reply. Finally in 1998 I decided to take the matter to court. All I needed a lawyer for on this occasion was mere formalities, nothing else. If it was possible to deal with the case alone this is how I would like to proceed, because that way I could be sure it would get processed. To know how pathetic and corrupt the Scottish legal system is, I was always very negative about the entire scenario, therefore repeatedly asked them in the office if they were prepared to take the case to court. This may seem obvious to most people but I had grave doubts, which did come to fruition. For what other reason would you employ a solicitor? These people are over-paid for the job they do, where I found it impossible for them to provide any service. In this instance, I was receiving legal aid but in other cases even paying them out of my pocket made no difference, as they still failed to do their required duty. As a final insult, these are in general pompous bloated people full of their own importance.

Correspondence began between the solicitors' office and the Social Services agency. Who, I had for a lawyer must have been skeptical about my claims when appearing rather surprised when what I was claiming produced evidence to support it on each occasion. The story he was given from this Government agency changed three or four different times corresponding with them being caught out giving fraudulent reasons as to why this claim ended. When it became certain, in their view, I was genuine about what I was saying, this was when the problems began. This is when it should have went to court...

It is not every day you find your solicitor hiding behind the door in his office when he should be attending to a client. Why did they take the case with the promise that it would go to court, and then try to hide like a child when the matter came to the crux? Thereafter, I was told as some type of recompense from another lawyer that the owner of the practice was taking his law exams and was about to become a judge, hence me being hung out to dry?! Saying, he didn't want to offend the legal establishment by dealing with a case involving a Government agency?! Whether this is true I don't know, but, what kind of law is that? What kind of judge will he make? What type of legal system is this? Any future cases with him will be the State is always right and you are always wrong - no matter what injustice is inflicted. This is in a country already brought to its knees solely for British Establishment oppression. Judging by this episode, with the ongoing complaint about how the British Government abusing human rights and inflict crimes against humanity, there can be no future hope for the nation.

The second of October 2000 I will always remember as the day Britain adopted new European Human Rights legislation. Once again I questioned this as a piece of hypocrisy, asking if Scots living in their country even have the right to the most fundamental human right; to life itself. Call it another coincidence or whatever, but it was to be expected that I should suffer more grave human rights violations on this day. I was independently witnessed being dragged out of my car by the hair in keeping with tradition for what was predicted for the second of October, the assailants being two police officers. After an altercation lasting over twenty-five minutes I was finally detained. At one point, when the officers responsible holding an arm each and at either side thrust me wholesale into the side of my car I did think to myself, 'Why won't you put dents in your police car in this manner?' It was all irrelevant, as I was assaulted, imprisoned, charged and hospitalized. This being another great day for human rights when they were supposed to be *enhanced*. For me, it was just a reminder of how bad it really is for the native people. From this incident onwards, just what happened next will shock you if my treatment doesn't already...

Excerpts of the following have previous been referred to in the text.

Personally, at the time I regarded the actual incident as routine such is my treatment. Maybe it would have been an advantage to have been colored then Scotland could have its own Rodney King!
All along, I maintained the officer most responsible was Scott Morrison of Central Police. When he was found dead on the sixth of November 2000 the six charges that appeared after were

allegedly fictitious. If the law does exist all five police officers named in this complaint should be charged with perverting the course of justice, and later contempt of court, if they produced false charges and statements. I wasn't holding my breath waiting for this to materialize.

I had been out of the country but on return I found my family had consulted a lawyer to *assist* with the case. On consulting this practice, I gave them the name of the police officer involved and told them there were no longer any charges against me because he was deceased. Not one to be fooled by untrustworthy solicitors I previously checked this legal point beforehand. All the lawyer/s needed to do was join the dots together – could it be any easier?

To have questioned a corrupt system for a long time, but in the present setting, if I was correct about what I was claiming, there was no viable way out of the predicament the five Strathclyde Police officers named in the complaint found themselves in. Corresponding with which, they declined to produce statements against me in connection with events from that night. This complemented my accusation they were not present at the time and place referred to. Finally, all their suspected corruption was about to be exposed yet nobody could ever comprehend just how corrupt the Scottish legal system really is. The judge wanted to proceed with this case even in absence of police statements, but it was my solicitor that argued against the integrity of the judge on the matter making a bizarre claim medical reports on mental health grounds were being sought in this case?! Such nonsense came out of the blue! However, by doing this, this bent lawyer made me look if I had some grave mental illness in the eyes of the judicial system. Further, he was opening the door to let the police off the hook at my expense! He was taking the case off at a tangent that (falsely and most definitely illegally) benefited the police (and also the Labour Government and Secret Service). It is always the small man who suffers in these situations... If I never had a solicitor 'acting' on my behalf this situation would never have arose and we could have proceeded to trial with the potential to expose some nasty practices.

I had witnesses to say I was the victim of a police assault, medical reports to confirm the injuries inflicted, I had given the

lawyers details of the police officers involved and later on a corresponding newspaper cutting on the death of Scott Morrison. What more did they need? Each time such details or information were presented to them it was met with a constant phrase, "That doesn't matter in this case!"
They blatantly told me they were going to stitch me up regardless of the evidence witnesses and truth?!

The newspaper story in the Daily Record 7/11/00 read:

Dead cop's 'bad times'

A YOUNG detective found dead in his car yesterday was under investigation for an alleged assault, it was revealed last night.
Father-of-two Constable Scott Morrison, 36, of Coals-naughton, Clackmannanshire, was also said to be going through 'bad times' with his wife.
His car was found at Shawpark Golf Club in Alloa.
He is believed to have died from carbon monoxide poisoning and police said his death was not being treated as suspicious.
His wife, Fiona, reported him missing on Monday.

There it was in black and white in a national newspaper stating who I claimed to be responsible, saying he was under investigation for an alleged assault. How much more confirmation did they need to substantiate what was being claimed? If this assault was not on me then who was it upon? Was it possible to manipulate the circumstances in any sense given the setting? What was the only viable alternative here; that the story was a figment of the journalist's imagination? I could produce other newspapers with the same story; did all those journalists share the same fantasy at the same time?
Of those other newspaper cuttings it said he had recently been promoted. Police officers do not get promotion when under investigation – i.e. this implies he was being set-up to take a fall?! He was possibly murdered?!

As time passed with continued postponement of the trial I was getting a bad feeling – although remaining blasé knowing full well it was the most corrupt circumstances imaginable - regarding this legal process before the ultimate betrayal materialized and questioned if these lawyers had been nobbled. There would be no surprise if this was so. There are many different ways to get at someone. The judge, to his credit, looked like the only honest person in the whole charade, and this is from me who is completely skeptical about Scots Law praising him! It was time to act, where now by this year you could access medical records so I researched them. What I found was astounding.

I had previously been given a clean bill of mental health by the dodgy psychiatrist, Dr Locke, whose records were now being studied. Every sentence written in these reports was fabricated to my detriment! Now I can't say that I am overly shocked at this because I'd previously been warned this would be the next tactic used against me, but what displeased me most was how I'd been caught out. Ever since my newspaper story materialized there was paramount need by them responsible to discredit what I was claiming, so I was always on guard for such an eventuality. What made me look silly more than anything else was how I honestly told people that I'd been to see a shrink who honestly found nothing wrong, exploding any possibility of a later deceit or any present insinuations of madness, only now at this final hour to find this skullduggery. Here is a sentence of what was used in the legal proceedings demonstrating what is being claimed: -

'He told me that he had seen this person as an alternative to asking for political asylum in Switzerland, a country out with the European Union (because the European Union was part of the cover-up conspiracy)'.

That psychiatrist was told the reason for applying for political asylum (if I had done so when there) in Switzerland was because you cannot get refugee status within the European Union in accordance with international law. She had manipulated the subject matter - all subject matter - to make me look like a fool when the reverse is obvious. This sentence, one example of many, was taken from a document used in Scottish legal proceedings for the benefit of legal professionals who should know this (if they have had legal training), yet they all chose to ignore it at a time when I repeatedly pointed out such fabrications and tactics! Alternatively, are they prepared to flout international law the way they do with their own corrupt piece of hypocrisy that passes for a legal system? When you consider these matters, in light of here is someone claiming he was being framed for murder (with evidence, and over ten million witnesses to support such claims), what hope have you if it went as far as a trial? Combine that with the guilty until proven innocent practice in operation. Lawyers, from whom I obtained the document, had been consistently told the truth but in their eagerness to rig the case they colluded in all this nonsense! In the end I remained curious to only one aspect concerning the way in which this injustice materialized; did they know in advance about the fabricated medical reports that were to be used against me? Is that why they pursued their inclusion into the legal procedures against the wishes of the judge? And if that is so; why did they do this?

I asked one of my solicitors if he had read the medical reports. He agreed he had - the above sentence from them is most appropriate to highlight this for it pertains to legal issues. I then asked if he'd seen all the fabrications to the extent what was written was madness on behalf of Dr Locke. He prevaricated upon being caught out lying once again...

Incidentally, it is a condition of being granted political asylum that you have to prove the law doesn't protect you in the country of persecution. As a final guarantee to being granted political asylum, to exhaust the process, I reported these lawyers to the Law Society. With ten serious complaints against them, the Society gave the most trivial lukewarm response, saying they were only prepared to take the most inconsequential of the ten complaints and offer to deal with it. I declined with this next affront but with which the corrupt system stays intact for they can claim to have a mechanism in place to deal with complaints, insulting as it is that nobody can get justice out of it.

When the court case was hijacked, it was stipulated the corrupt psychiatrist, Dr Locke, be used to give a second medical opinion - independent that would be! Of course this would be so, for they couldn't trust the judgment of another...

From this minor road traffic incident where all this aspires from; here is a list of crimes I allege to have occurred in connection with which.

1. I faced six fictitious charges: I always claimed Scott Morrison was most responsible and after his death there were no charges to answer to. I previously checked what passes for a law to make certain of this, but my lawyers pursued a different agenda against my protestations.
2. I was the victim of an assault: Independent witnesses claimed I was dragged from the car then assaulted. At the time I had very little to say on the subject but others spoke up in my defense and hospital bandages were apparent on my body afterwards.
3. I was wrongfully arrested and detained: All I was trying to do that night was drive home. The next time I was arrested, my crime was that of walking in a public park, yet they fabricated charges against me for that also.
4. I was the victim of an attempted murder: Who I believed to be Special Branch ran a speeding car at me five days before what should have been the actual trial. This was again independently witnessed. When the car was driven towards me at high speed, I was in a corridor between my vehicle and a cemented garden wall that was too high to jump over. Where to survive this a first gigantic step was straight towards the oncoming speeding car thereby reducing the distance, then sidestepping with a fraction of a second to spare, to step behind my vehicle. All I felt at the time was the wind turbulence off their car wing mirror. After over four years of other such incidents survival becomes impulsive. [If you were to be hit by a speeding vehicle, the trick is to jump into the air, thereby reducing the likelihood of breaking bones. I even had my own medical care arranged for such an eventuality because I was not going to trust the predicted practice of lying in the nearest hospital in these circumstances.]
5. I was the victim of an attempted blackmailing: The psychiatrist claimed she had an offer from the Procurator

Fiscal (the legal service agency behind the courts) where, if I accepted medication all six charges would be dropped. This offer was based upon the mental illness she'd just fabricated. All six charges disappeared without either conforming to the system or being tricked by this dubious practitioner. A lesser person would have panicked and then taken what appeared to be the softer option of accepting her illegal medicine. [It would have been so easy to fake consumption of medication but I refused to go down that route for I was in the right when up against them that operate in defense of evil pedophiles - you have to live with yourself first of all!]

6. Falsified documents were used in legal proceedings: The same psychiatrist that tried to blackmail me was the very person who admitted I had no mental deficiency whatsoever, then unable to justify the lies told they continually changed the medical reports depending on who or for what purpose they were to be used in an attempt to cover-up what she'd done.

7. The death of Scott Morrison had a major question mark placed over it: The night of the road traffic incident, without trying to sound threatening, I hinted to this officer someone would be in serious trouble for what had happened. At the time, I resigned myself to accept that I would be murdered such was the prevailing scenario. Morrison was later found dead and the newspaper story appeared in print on my birthday – another nasty coincidence. His family, sore at his loss, were phoning me to complain until the calls started getting blocked! If only they knew the truth; I tried to save his life that night but he was on a power-trip and not prepared to listen.

8. Perverting the course of justice: Six fictitious charges, a lawyer that betrays his client, an attempted murder to prevent the trial taking place; this could go on and on, need I say any more?

9. Contempt of court: Had I behaved in the same manner as what those five Strathclyde Police officers did by continually refusing to submit what was requested, this is what I would have been charged with early on in proceedings. They can do this and then go unpunished every time.

10. Intimidating witnesses: Strathclyde Police appeared to be offering a new crime to their repertoire of terror, intimidating suspects, when they sent Special Branch after me before the trial began.

{There are probably just as many other crimes connected that are not listed here.}

I'd never been in court since I decided to fight the oppression by telling the truth with the original tactic four years previous. The only other incident that could have placed me there was when I refused to produce motoring documents, but this was ignored other than one trick telephone call I refused to answer. What did it natter, they could stick me in court, it was only going to cost them in terms of reputation with the potential to annoy more people in the hope some kind of justice could materialize, and with it I would get another £50 fine – money well spent as far as I was concerned because I desperately needed the publicity. Likewise, I wanted compensation to again highlight what was occurring, but this never materialized due to these crooked lawyers. The present scenario was most acute, as the authorities were already aware that I knew about the present First Minister being associated with a death that could possibly have him charged with conspiracy to murder. I couldn't make it any more obvious for I promoted the fact by naming him in my infamous e-book *Who Killed Jill Dando*. Further, what is undeniable is, he had been promoted to lead the Labour Party in Scotland after the incident in which the Special Branch agent was killed. Is there any sense of shame to these people? Could they afford to have me telling the truth with the potential to reveal such an awkward setting? Who knows what would be revealed? Exposure of Henry McLeish and allegedly associated murders had to be avoided at all costs because no sane person could ever vote in favor of such. They had done so in the past unbeknown, but voters will be alarmed at what they lend their support to and how they were conned into doing so once the truth materializes.

To falsely certify someone insane is one thing, but to do it with over ten million witnesses verifying their story is another, not that the Government, Strathclyde Police or the Secret Service ever cared a damn for reality for they have a propaganda machine at their disposal to convince the ignorant masses of any falsehood. Furthermore, I am someone who in the past has educated a university professor in his own subject and have, with various examples, proven myself to be the best in the world at what I do, all of this is combined with praise from the best.

When they cannot answer to a situation (I don't foresee them ever answering to this, especially with what would appear to be a secret agenda to destroy anything that resembles a law) it is simply ignored. The law is not going to have them stand trial never mind punish them. McLeish, for a good example, was supposedly removed from Office concerning his dodgy deeds in connection with sub-letting constituency offices but criminal charges never materialized?!

Now it may be asked why I never changed solicitors, but to who? When the entire system is conspiring against you; whose going to stand up to it? This is a country where two Glasgow lawyers have been found dead in suspicious circumstances plus another from the Scottish Executive. Maybe a lot more...

Likewise, given it is impossible for me to get to any court, for their attempted murder on this occasion was also ignored when I asked for it to be processed given I had an independent witness prepared to give testimony on my behalf, thereby it is pointless trying to take this case to the European Court of Human Rights (ECHR) for I would only be murdered to prevent it being heard.

Now I question Scots Law because it is unbelievably corrupt but the two cases concerning me in England were the double murder of Lin and Megan Russell and the killing of celebrity Jill Dando. In both a patsy was in place, myself for the double murder, and, Dr Alan Farthing for his soon-to-be wife. Neither attempt was successful, but in both cases another innocent person was convicted!

Warrants with fabricated intelligence in them to justify my illegal persecution are signed at 11 Church Street Belfast.

I was a victim of the Milly Dowler telephone hacking scandal but was denied compensation because the case against me was ongoing – again, based upon fabricated intelligence in their reports.

Lord Advocate Frank Mulholland, refused to process the guilty claiming the case was under investigation. The same case a UN representative described as genocide. Frank was predictably awarded a CBE from the Queen.

A constant tactic of the police was to arrest another innocent person every time the truth started to emerge to prevent any political or independent investigation, even when the actual killer was named. Afterwards, he said he would refuse to deal with me and put any future correspondence 'on file' – whatever that means?! The nearest thing to an admission of guilt was when it was claimed 'other agencies were involved in this!' Of course they were, MI5 having a policy of mass murder then MI5 overseeing the investigations?!

The SNP took power then when wanting to demonstrate trust with the people/sheople kept Mulholland in position. When they finally replaced him I found the *Royal Mail* no longer functions for a letter I sent was returned. The postman/postwoman couldn't find the Scottish Parliament?!

'Fear not the serpent who bears false witness against you.'

8. POLITICS.

'It was one of those nights, we had been at the country club playing snooker but when I got back to the car the doors that had been locked was now unlocked. When I went to switch on the car radio it all lit up, which it never did before. Someone had obviously been in the car trying to steal the radio, but had in fact done such a good job of repairing it, had I known this was going to happen, I would have left a set of spanners with a note saying

what else needed mending. Anyway, undeterred we ventured into town to finish off the night. There we met Logan. A victim I thought. After all, Logan was a 'hard-man' and if you are going to victimize someone it had to be either a policeman, a politician or a hard-case. There is no fun in picking on anyone else that cannot get you killed or jailed. This was the same character who once set my hair on fire in the school bus, but now at twenty-six-years-old, married with a son but remained terrified of his father, and still he pursued the hard-man image?! It was a Sunday night, Logan was drunk and couldn't return home because he was afraid his father would give him a kicking because he was not capable of going to his work in the morning. My devious mind worked overtime on this. I had to see his father give him a good kicking, he needed to grow up, given it was the best policy. He might even thank me for it in later life – but I doubt it. I did all the planning right in front of him. Where else would you, him being the victim? Then, when the drunk Logan asked for a lift home I was only too delighted to oblige. Beside me in the car was Debbie in the passenger seat, with Simon and Logan in the back where the destination was a farm past the row of houses in which both Logan and his father separately lived. On the hill going up to the row of houses I started to jump up and down on the accelerator pedal to imitate that the car was running low on fuel. Simon in the back seat gave a rehearsed, "What's wrong with the car?"

"It's running out of petrol," was the stage-managed reply.

We turned off the main road to intentionally break down right outside Logan's father's house praying Logan would never see the petrol gauge indicating that the tank was quarter full. Unknown to me, the row of houses was on a downward slope and it was simply impossible to stop at the chosen spot. The car rolled on and on, I had to think quickly so in desperation I jumped on the brake pedal to enact a sudden halt. The only thing was, there was no parcel shelf in the car and in doing so the entire interior lit up luminous red. It never registered with the hard-man what I'd done, so we could continue with the plan unabated. He was just too drunk. Suddenly his drunkenness subsided when he realized where we were parked with, "What's wrong with the car?"

"Its ran out of petrol; I told you we were short of petrol," was my predicable response.
At this myself and Simon alighted from the vehicle and started arguing loudly, "It's all your fault, I told you we were short of petrol."
"You're driving the car, it's your fault."
"You were the one wanting to play snooker."
"You were the one wanting to go into town."
On and on we argued edging closer to the father's house with every shout and curse getting louder. Debbie, as instructed, rolled down the passenger window and let out a girly shriek, "Yous pair of bastards want to cut that out."
As we got closer to the house to intentionally wake up Logan's father, the hard-man went white with fear cowering in the backseat, then finally he asked Debbie, "Why don't they just hit each other?"
In the end a shaken Logan emerged from the car before any sign of his father appeared. He made for both of us, grabbing each by the lapels with both his hands. Addressing Simon first he said, "You want to keep the noise down; you might wake my father."
At, 'you might wake my father,' I nearly wet myself with the contortions my body was taking trying not to laugh out loud. He turned on me next, my torso shaking uncontrollably so with a face that couldn't hide the humor any more when he asked, "What's wrong with you? Why are you laughing?"
I had to think quickly and come up with a blinder of an answer, therefore replied, "I have just remembered, I have a can full of petrol in the back of the car."
The night finished off with me deliberately splashing some petrol over my hands and over the side of the car so to bring the smell inside when off we drove to the farm.'

It was probably during the miners' strikes of the nineteen-eighties British democracy died. The truth is, it must have been dead long beforehand that I could accurately see and so confidently predict as a schoolboy, 'They (the miners) will never win,' when confronting the Government of Thatcher. I suppose this was when English democracy died, but to have been a Scot who had never known what democracy was, it presumably went in Scotland when oil was discovered there. If it ever existed previously. From early times, this nation was always regarded as a valuable commodity for English nobles to exploit with everything from gold to intellectual property where the country was repeatedly plundered and her citizens butchered over the last millennium. Today, here was oil English elites wanted to exploit; what would they care for the native citizens in such a situation? Is it any different in Iraq in recent times? The probable only real difference is, it is all done in a subtle manner in Western countries, such as my uncle's experience in *Questionable Motives* where the truth of the matter is nearly impossible to obtain. Only now do others look back and realize Thatcher ruined the country. She was never going to give in to those miners because that meant compromise and she was not known for such. Her famous phrase demonstrates this attitude (from another incident); 'The lady's not for turning'. When the Conservative Party left Office they left a massive debt of over fifty billion in sterling that continues to be paid back even to this day, yet 'Thatcher's miracles' produced many millionaires. This being prior to the banking crash they were instrumental in creating raising the debt to trillions. For most British in the nineteen-eighties wealth mainly came to them through a property boom, not that the country was ever producing goods under Conservative rule to justify this wealth. It was the policies of a lunatic regime. She was in power at the end of the Cold War, where instead of reducing the budget for the Secret Service it doubled! With all that wealth and those responsible no longer employed in their original task, of course it would be ordinary citizens that suffered. People were targeted for little or no reason where those responsible answered to nobody plus there is no recourse open to the aggrieved – the only way out of this predicament for me is death. The higher the standing of the individual the more likely they were to be spied upon. Politicians were also victims, where it was handy for the upper echelons of power to have something held over the minions so they could be manipulated when the need arose. Many allegations of pedophile and concealed homosexuality exist against many in high society that could be used for blackmailing purposes. In at least one instance MI5 were alleged to be responsible for supplying the rent-boys. It can all be denied, but this period of change could be viewed as the end of British democracy.

The wife of a former Prime Minister (Cherie Blair) is said to have a personal file with the Secret Service, as has Blair's former right-hand-man Peter Mandelson.

Leadership of Thatcher was replaced by John Major. Under whose rule the Labour leader, John Smith, was allegedly murdered and passed off as a heart attack to prevent him becoming Prime Minister, as I was informed from the inside! Major was relatively ineffectual compared to his predecessor, therefore it was just more of the same but with a human face to it. The Conservatives were finally ousted in 1997 by the Labour Party led by Tony Blair. For certain, he never restored any measure of human rights for I suffered the majority of my persecution and many suspicious deaths occurred under his regime. During that year there was arguably three attempts to frame me for murder (of them I could name suspects for every case, not that that was ever a concern to the guilty parties) and a visit from the Men in Black amongst other nasty things. At the 1997 election, no Conservative MPs were returned to the British Parliament from Scotland such was their dreadful record there. Instead, the people were fooled into voting for an alternative nightmare, the Labour Party, otherwise referred to as the red Tories. In relation to the terror campaign, all that really changed was the color of the election manifesto.

Of interest is the murder of Tracey Wilde where I named an alleged killer in my 'Press release'. The Scottish National Party were at that time the official opposition party where a prominent member was wrongly associated with her murder (part of the dirty tricks campaign the Secret Service orchestrate against nationalist politicians), where I frustrated the situation and what I found was irrefutable evidence the Labour Party were at the very least indirectly associated with this crime! No public broadcast stating this was ever made – nor likely to until democracy, human rights and law are restored. The murder of Tracey Wilde was just one of many suspicious deaths. Now you may have a better idea relating to how the Unionist parties operate, where such treachery can use be to obtain then retain power!

Facts and figures about Scotland are quite astonishing. Seventy to seventy-five percent of the oil produced in Europe comes from Scottish waters. In addition to which there is gas, coal, gold, other minerals, fishing, farming, forestry and many other industries. This small nation is undoubtedly the richest in Europe for natural resources. Officially it is rated around the seventh richest country in the world. Seventy percent of the best inventions came from Scottish inventors - from the television to the pedal bicycle. In contrast to all this potential wealth, it consistently has the worst housing schemes in Europe; the Kingston Bridge was the busiest stretch of road in Britain; when the Fraser's Building stood on Argyll Street Glasgow it had the highest business rates in Britain; Glasgow has the titles of being the 'murder capital of Europe' and 'heroin capital of Europe'; and finally to complete the dastardly picture, Edinburgh was called the 'AIDS capital of Europe' in the nineteen-eighties. On official figures Scots are twice more likely to be under Secret Service surveillance than their English counterparts. This being official figures that have been known to change depending upon the situation, so it could be a lot higher! In recent times Scotland has the highest emigration rate of any Western country, which makes it the fastest diminishing population in Europe. So, what is happening here?

From North Sea oil revenue, an estimation of over £160 billion has been drained out of the country with the people suffering a further indignity of being called 'subsidy junkies' by an English MP. This figure was taken twelve years back so the actual figure is far higher. Further, such a value simply does not add up. For Norway, with a fraction of the oil reserves, built up a national oil fund of £600 billion. What is certain is, if Scots had kept their wealth there would be no subsidy junkies. Robbed and then insulted and oppressed for it. When the national bard, Robert Burns, wrote about the Scottish ruling classes being in cahoots with the English ruling classes:

'We were bought and sold for English gold, Such a parcel of rogues in a nation.' Today it would be more accurate if he wrote, *'We were bought and sold for <u>Scottish</u> gold, Such a parcel of rogues in a nation.'*

For it is their wealth that is paying for the corrupt circumstances.

With natural resources alone making it head and shoulders the richest country in Europe, people should be desperate to live there instead of leaving by droves. Luxembourg became the richest country in the world, but a propaganda campaign used in Scotland said it is too small to be independent, but in reality it is geographically fifty times larger than this tiny Benelux nation. With what is arguably the most talented people on this planet - such ingenuous still exists – combined with the wealth the land holds it is impossible to fail business wise. No other country can boast of such a winning economic formula. In light of this, I was just another example of how impossible it is to succeed there. For example, what at the time was the most advanced production engine in the world had many design faults, but when I seen the plans for it in a magazine I knew exactly what was wrong and how to fix it. A Doctor of engineering at Caledonian University that I keep in touch with, I wrote and detailed out what was wrong knowing he often worked for the company responsible. Design faults were detailed out, what the symptoms would be, and, noted was what needed to be done to cure the problems. All of which said proved accurate to the letter. It was a combination of knowledge and having a feel for the engine without ever seeing it that led me to being so accurate in this projected prognosis. Unbeknown, he had this engine in his possession but had to return it because he was unable to solve the problems. This happened a week before I contacted him. In the end I went to the importer, where, with my guidance, the most successful version was produced in England. Unfortunately, this was at a time when the company was already bankrupt so it all came to nothing. I obviously had the talent for this knowing I could achieve what the factory after many years of struggle and at least two universities and two development companies failed to with all their massive budgets resources and supposed expertise. This case is not a sole example of my talent, whereby I was possibly the best in the world at what I do - such could pose problems when the psychiatrist, Dr Locke, repeatedly fabricated medical records to say I was insane, and, likewise, the corrupt legal system that relied upon such nonsense to deny me justice and compensation yet have the murders in Strathclyde continue!

Instead of assisting others for little or no gratification, I was determined to start in business. Here was an ability that proved unsurpassed. The determination was there. I put in the long hours and had enough money to make it possible. No, I could not fail, but I was neglecting one incurable ill. I was a Scot living at home who wanted to succeed there. Such is not allowed, for they will fail you. And, yes, they did. All along I harbored reservations since being a schoolboy about how repressive it is, only to later have what was suspected materialize as an adult. Although I was always alert, the difference between me and any other native citizen was I was so far ahead of the competition, so brilliant, that I believed I could overcome any deliberately imposed obstacle. The truth is, it so utterly repressive and all done so subtly you would not expect it.

My story is curious when you consider I had already proven to be the best in the world in various fields, genuinely wanted to improve the conditions of my fellow citizen, yet it is me who gets a visit from the Men in Black. It is me who gets targeted for murders where the actual suspects and others associated are found dead. It is me who was left looking at thirty-five years in a prison cell for crimes I didn't commit. It is me who has every wrongful stigma against my name - from being a pedophile to a godfather of crime. It is me who is left penniless unable to access the money owed. Another curious aspect in all this is I worked on engine technology, which invariably was to help the environment by means of creating less pollution and greater efficiency. The morons responsible have no concern whatsoever for creating a better world that is less contaminated. Instead they are engrossed in their stupid little boy's games for which we will all suffer sooner or later. Those Gulf Wars created enormous pollution and wastage of oil reserves; for what? For certain Western countries to dominate the world's oil supply (although previously hinted at in the text is what they really seek). Soldiers suffering from (denied cause of) Gulf War Syndrome suspect depleted uranium used in shells to be responsible. Again, another type of pollution done by Western forces.

All that talent, living in one of the richest countries in the world but this is how it really is. I can give other examples of this being the case if you think these circumstances are isolated. Do Scots fight this oppression? What do Scots fight for? Do Scots even bother themselves to fight?

Ones that do fight align themselves to the conflict in Ireland/Northern Ireland as either Loyalist or Republican terrorists. Others are in the security forces or the British Army. They wrap themselves up in religious ideology fighting for the 'cause' but live the most deprived lives at home. Is it any wonder this country had the highest emigration rate in the Western World! This is idiot nation at its worst.

After the plane crashes on the World Trade Centre Saddam Hussein was the only world leader to allegedly praise these attacks. This was not a wise thing to do in the circumstances. He being leader of a country with the second largest oil reserves in the world (Saudi Arabia has the largest) insulting the only remaining super-power. What would be the outcome?

I was looking at the situation questioning the authenticity of the New York attacks with some personal insight of world politics. Such as, I had grown up close to the Clyde Estuary, which contains the largest untapped and easiest accessible oil reserves in Europe hence the prevailing scenario, where Scots have already suffered a theft of billions in oil reserves from the North Sea, or in the words of the Scottish National Party, 'The only country in the world ever to discover oil and then become poorer for it'. Was the second grand theft underway? The city of Glasgow sits at the head of the Clyde Estuary to once have a population of over a million. Now, it only has just over half that. This is the city of mass suicides in the River Clyde that suddenly stopped when a woman reported a man had tried to throw her into the water. The city with outbreaks of Anthrax among junkies where the press claim this agent of biological warfare is common in opium! Only when the affected heroin started killing people further afield, like in Dublin, was any real concern shown on the matter! Is that because the problem had spread to a territory not under British control to cover up what was happening? By this time, Anthrax was no longer reported as such – nobody knows what it was supposed to be then! Glasgow is the city where prostitutes are strangled on Sunday nights/Monday mornings but no serial killer operates there (according to the police) even with the suspects being regularly found dead! Suspects in the loosest term of the word. Plus, a multitude of other suspicious deaths…

Saddam Hussein was accused of operating a repressive regime, but far worst exist. Where, for him to praise the World Trade Center attacks was surely folly. Saddam was a tyrant, but maybe he should have kept his thoughts quiet. What it gave the United States was a pretext to attack Iraq, although they had never stopped attacking the country since the first Gulf War. A claim prior to the second Gulf conflict that he possessed weapons of mass destruction (WMD) has been proven unfounded, this, and George Bush Junior saying, "This man tried to kill my daddy." Were these reasons really justification for war?

'Winston Churchill had the machine-guns turned on the striking workers in George Square, Glasgow, after the Great War.'

9. THE AUTHORITIES.

'A letter appeared Friday morning stating I should appear in the Social Security office at 11:30AM on the Monday concerning my claim for unemployment benefit. At the time I had been working so hard and such long hours I slept in and appeared at the later

time of 12 noon; tying shoe laces and buttoning up my shirt inside the office. When it was my turn to see the clerk I said apologetically, "Sorry I'm late but I slept in, will I come back another time?"

This was met with a stern, "No, we want you in the office now, Mr. Rae."

Totally oblivious to what was going on, I was sent into a room I had never been in before to be interviewed by a woman I'd never seen before. When she said she had a complaint about myself for working while claiming benefit, only then did I realize what was happening; I had been grassed in for working when on the dole. No panic, it is all very simple, you just answer no to every question and if they don't have hard evidence to prove you were working while claiming benefit you walk out of there a free man. To most people this is the well practiced strategy. Only, here was I working night and day and didn't know which particular job I had to answer for, so that strategy might get me caught out. Come on; was I really going to lie to these people over a measly £40 a week, turn into some form of snake for that, you must be out of your mind if you think I would stoop that low. The attractive woman began her line of questioning with, "Have you be working, Mr. Rae?"

Unequivocally, "YES", thinking to myself that would impress her.

She lit up in disbelief at such honesty thinking she had finally caught someone for once instead of chasing shadows making her pointless profession worthwhile. She continued with, "What have you been working at, Mr. Rae?"

"I've been doing my engineering."

"Oh, we didn't know about that, where are you doing your engineering, Mr. Rae?"

"At the workshop in Cumnock, it's in your records."

"I didn't know about that," she replied.

On it continued in this manner where instead of answering no to every question I answered yes to all until it became a fishing exercise.

"Have you been working on a farm, Mr Rae?"

Again came the unequivocal, "YES."

"When were you working on a farm, Mr. Rae?"

"When I was fifteen-years-old."
All along she'd been writing down the answers with every 'Yes' said only to score them all back out again once an explanation was granted.
Finally, "You can go now, Mr. Rae."
I was very disgruntled thinking this interrogation was only just warming up, so asked sullenly, "What, is that it?"
Tears in her eyes, she pointed at the door and started screaming in a high pitched voice, "WILL YOU PLEASE JUST LEAVE NOW."
At this I left bewildered wondering who was in the most trouble, me or her? I also had a day's work to do.'

At this point I had been convicted of attacking three people and a big dog with a baseball bat where a social worker sat opposite writing down a background report on my circumstances, when he nonchalantly asked, "How do you feel about what you have done, Mr. Rae?"
This, a standard enough question asked of every convicted person before sentencing. He must have heard, 'It was totally out of character of me,' a thousand times before, as he expected me to hear something along these lines (the other favorite, when doing time, is to let God into your life!). How did I feel about what I had done? As a family, it wasn't safe to live in our home such was the prevailing situation we found ourselves in. We'd been attacked in our home by six men previously and reported it to the police, at the time naming who was responsible and the registration number of one of the cars involved, but nothing was done about it other than being laughed at by the police, as was always the case. When who I recognized as being responsible returned to do the same again four years later what were my options? I never denied breaking his car window that day though I would dispute every other aspect of this conviction. So when that social worker asked that question he received an honest answer when I steadfastly maintained, "I did the right thing."
His pen stuck in the page in the middle of the word he was writing. He looked up astonished and fearful for his life at what he believed to be a psychopath sitting within striking distance. Only a desk separated us. Him sitting there with only a tiny pen

to defend himself with. It was he who asked the stupid question; in the circumstances, what did he expect me to say?

The truth is I had been a victim of the never ending State terror and oppression once too often – all my life. This is all the citizens have ever known therefore most accept it as the norm. Yes, I did the right thing especially so when I considered a friend who never where the same family responsible nearly killed him twice. The first time he was beaten and slashed then later shot and I had never suffered neither, nor would it happen twice. I told him many times what he needed to do but of course he never heeded the advice given. So, instead of scaring social workers who help preserve the corrupt system, he went off to intensive care twice. You make your own decisions and I'd obviously made the right one even if it meant being convicted and persecuted by a corrupt system. Did this social worker really think I was going to kiss ass in these circumstances?

As for the police (irrespective of involvement in the above mentioned scenarios), here is an amusing story to demonstrate how they provide no service whatsoever but are constantly present to oppress people. A friend, who is a keen angler, wanted me to telephone the local police regarding poachers at the reservoir to which he is a member of the adjoining club. In the end, after offering him the telephone and what other methods I could think of to avoid making this call (and the repercussions of) I finally did. The moment I picked up the receiver I was certain of two things; one, they would do nothing of what is asked of them, and two; I would become a victim for inconveniencing them just by giving them a crime to investigate.

Well, after promising they would go and catch the poachers in twenty minutes, this mate waited for them to appear, but of course I was right when certain they would have no intention of, and needless to say they never did bother themselves. He then made the mistake of complaining saying he'd waited for them for hours but they never appeared only to receive the reply I was a, 'Lying bastard' because they claimed I never called. He was adamant this was not the case for he and two others stood behind me listening into the conversation at the time. How predictable it was, as ever the police provided no service whatsoever yet attack however asks them to actually do something; the supposed duty for which they are employed. When this mate came back saying they called me a lying bastard upon being blissfully aware of the truth, he found it strange I was not offended in the least but fell about laughing. I knew what to expect. There would only have been surprise if they did honor their word and went and caught the poachers in twenty minutes! This story is one of the least offensive I can think of to give as an example. It is also one of the least damning. Where I'd been full of dread making the call knowing the jeopardy it could place myself in, wondering at the time what would happen to me, but in the end only a wrongful insult materialized. I certainly got off lightly on this occasion.

There is something fundamentally wrong about a system where you know in advance how bad it is only to have this verified upon consulting it.

I have constantly wondered why or for what purpose the police – as public servants - really operate. Tax-payers pay for a service they simply do not get, yet nobody is allowed to criticize them as they become a victim of police harassment and/or brutality after. They must spend a fortune of tax-payers' money maintaining a public image of respectability when the public are aware of how corrupt it really is. They are self-serving only furthering their power, presence and objectives never answering to the public but only to themselves and London masters. Further, they don't answer to the law, which is where the problem lies...

Every police force in Britain has a Special Branch attached. These men and women are independent of routine investigations, drugs offenses and most serious crimes. Their supposed duty is to deal with offenses concerning national security, in particular terrorism. This is all very well, but when there is little or no threat towards the nation, and from expansion under the Government of Thatcher to present times, in Scotland there has no longer been a threat since the mid-nineties, so what are they doing to justify their existence?

I was once at a commemoration service for William Wallace (aka *Braveheart*) where of the handful present to make up the small crowd there were Special Branch agents included. I purposely positioned myself at the rear to see all present. It was obvious they had little or no purpose for Wallace has been dead for over seven hundred years and the famous folk singer, Anne Lorne Gilles, speaking didn't appear threatening in any sense. Was she really going to inspire a rebellion with one of her love songs?

'...will ye go lassie go, and we'll all go together, to pick wild mountain tyne all around the blooming heather...'

Unintentionally I was at one of Scotland's prestige golf clubs prior to a celebrity tournament of the rich and famous when I spotted what I believed to be Special Branch being active. Scotland is the home of golf and can be sold around the world in such a manner to attract influential people to these events. But, what were the security people up to? Special Branch in favored *BT* (British Telecom) vans appeared to be wiring up the course! I thought about it, national security, which is their supposed duty is not achieved in this manner. Obviously they were operating beyond their remit. The more I pondered the subject the more disturbed I became. It was acceptable to the governing elites for these people to abuse the Scottish nation with their antics, as is their habit, where nearly everything done are grave human rights violations with little or no justification, but what was happening here appeared to be beyond that. Were they staging these sporting spectaculars to include some of the most influential people in this world solely to obtain information? The chosen few allowed to play are by invitation only. Are they then paired up into cordial groups to make conversation easy? Let out onto a golf course, in the pretense of it being an open field, therefore free from eavesdropping to disclose intimate details with compatible acquaintances that are then secretly recorded?

With my record and experiences with Special Branch I left in a hurry. I had seen enough! Now, the rich and famous spend a lot of money on personal security plus value their privacy, therefore they would feel somewhat betrayed if this is how they are being mistreated. As a nation it is flaunted for whatever purpose suits the ruling Establishment in London where any implications can always be made appear fall on the native people. What if the good and the great become suspicious of underhand practices just as I had become and then started refusing invitations to the home of golf in the splendor of rural Scotland? How would the authorities explain that away? Perhaps, a terrorist outbreak? Those nasty Scots at it again…

An IRA member told about similar antics being conducted. At the Irish border customs post he maintained they put microphones up in the trees above the vehicles. Left stationary for a period with the window rolled down to show passports military intelligence could listen into conversations of occupants' incognito!

What I once seen being done on a golf course does not compare with the allegation about President Donald Trump on his visit to the United Kingdom. He was on the golfing range when he was allegedly attacked by a pulse energy weapon killing a bodyguard. Why was this assassination attempt never front-page news the world over? And, given he was previously a victim of British MI6 spy Christopher Steele with a faked dossier on Russian collusion, which was allegedly paid for by those close to Hillary Clinton to destroy his election prospects, at what point does America justifiably declare war on the United Kingdom for such treachery? The weapon allegedly used is the sole property of a national government?! The easiest way of determining which is to consider in which country was it being operated? Later, once he returned to the US, a politician was loudly making a jibe about Trump being on the golf course, said in an aggressive manner, i.e. threatening the President in a subtle manner though few would know what was being insinuated?! Did this speaker know the truth yet it was being concealed from the general public?

Special Branch can be considered the eyes and the ears of MI5 covering all aspects of society, in particular, airports and harbors in conjunction with customs officers. Furthermore, Special Branch usually are the hands that carry out the dirty work for MI5. Whereas MI5 itself is likened to the FBI. Both are charged with domestic security duties within their respective countries. Because MI5 operate against the Provisional IRA and the INLA, they are also allocated responsibility for covering all of Ireland.

MI6 is akin to the CIA, it being a worldwide operation spreading its tentacles into the most contentious of places. From a throwback to the British Empire, MI6 are said to have the best international network of any spy agency. Does that still hold true?

'Never trust a snake-charmer.'

10. CHARACTERS.

'I had taken Simon fishing into the Highlands, but this was never a serious pursuit for either of us. Once the fishing was over instead of driving straight home, we, in our best traditions, would take the long way, only in doing so the car developed a puncture. Stationary in the middle of the mountains both of us got out and looked around thinking more seriously now; where was the nearest pub? Pub; there wasn't even houses out here never mind a population to drink in a public house. Crest-fallen we would have to repair the car. Then I spied it, a big black Mercedes car approaching in the distance, so said to Simon, "Start a fight."
"Start a fight? The car is broken down; we don't even know where we are, and you want to start a fight. You are fucking mad."
After a quick explanation, the two of us started roaring and swearing at each other, him armed with the car-jack and me armed with the wheel-brace we started swinging them at each other. The big black flashy car passed slowly with the occupants visible faces stuck to the side windows looking at two mad characters stranded in the middle of nowhere fighting with each other. It passed, and then accelerated into the distance. We both collapsed in hysterics afterwards.'

My old grandfather never gave an inch until his dying day. I can still remember him in that hospital bed (probably for the only time in his life), which sat in the corner with a golden glow of light over the sheets. A hard stern old man humiliated in the end by being attended to with nurses. Nurses, he often assured me in the past, which were nothing more than back-scratchers and bed-changers. As he raised up his hand with the last drop of energy he possessed so I would take it but unfortunately I never did. A fact that always haunted me?! Was it me that was cold and heartless, or was this me adhering to his standards? Do you ever take another man's hand even if it is them closest to you? Where did the coldness come from?

His eldest son lost his only child, divorced his wife, lost his car and driving license, his house and job. After all this he often joked about his dog dying on him. With which, he was already an alcoholic and then attempted suicide, but not a single word of sympathy from my grandfather. Instead he made derogatory remarks at his failings. Dear God, did life ever deal someone such a losing hand and all his father could see in the situation was weakness. I was different, I always thought the world of my uncle and still do; I always will.

From diagnosing the above; maybe I relate to others how they relate to me…

On leaving the hospital scene that day with my mother driving the car, she optimistically tried to keep spirits high as she made plans for her father. She was falsely reassuring herself he'd be okay. I had seen this situation once before and found it one of the most tragic, when you can't tell a woman that she is hoping against all hope, as the man only had hours to live. Hours later he passed away, just as presumed. Death is something I accept as being part of the cycles of nature therefore I have fewer emotions towards it.

For all my grandfather's uncompromising attitude and his strict nature, he was far from being a moron. The man was a craftsman in his profession. I heard him tell his welding stories about how skilled and dedicated he was. Years later, I would learn to weld and loved it, even when it all went wrong to be showered in molten metal and I wanted to scream the building down but instead continued on to finish the weld. When people close to you die, in general, they leave you with something to cherish. Granddad left me with a story I carried through life: -

The family used to collect insurance money for the Co-Operative. Once this money accumulated within the house my grandfather's brother, Jim, stole it and ran off to join the Royal Air Force (RAF). This happened just before the Second World War broke out, where brother Jim became successful earning his *Wings* for flying. Granddad, on the other hand, was ordered by the Ministry of Defense (MoD) to stay at home because he was of more use to the country working in his father's blacksmith's shop producing specialized chains without a joint in them for war-ships. When the conflict ended his brother came home to the town of Auchinleck from where he left in disgrace. He proudly marched up the street with his chest puffed out in an RAF uniform with *Wings* and medals dangling from it. All the neighbors in the street turned out to see him return. At which, my grandfather would say in a thick Scots accent "Aye; he came home a bloody hero."

To me that one little story puts life in a nutshell. Things are never as they seem on the surface especially with those who have a need to promote themselves. Who are the bloody heroes? There are few heroes when you get right down to it. We are all cowards in some respect. The ones who tell you different are either lying or insane, or failing that both. In general it is usually the wife men fear the most!

As a schoolboy I can remember when Bobby Sands starved himself to death in the Maze Prison in 1981. Back then, we never had a television and I was not from a family that promoted the religious divide (Catholic/Protestant) having grown up never knowing what particular sect of Christianity we were, so it remained somewhat mysterious as to what it was really about. On the school bus there were the sick jokes at the time about Bobby Sands, such as: What was Bobby Sands' telephone number? The answer being, 808080 (ate nothing, ate nothing, ate nothing).
 Only now do I realize it is the Secret Service that promote such depraved behavior; yes, even to school kids who don't know any better. What I never would have believed back then was twenty years later I would be living in Ireland, drinking in an Irish pub

and reading an Irish broadsheet newspaper on the anniversary of Sands' death that detailed his story and I was crying tears, now knowing exactly how he felt. To have been in the position that I was left starving to the extent my stomach rejected food when I received some, or when my entire forehead burst open and bled for six weeks for no reason, I had also suffered every indignity imaginable. This was from someone who had never cried a tear in their adult life until I turned thirty. To have been Scottish I had grown up under the same oppression Thatcher imposed on the Province of Ulster, only the world didn't really know about the Irish oppression until Sands died, after which it became well published, but Scotland never had such an event to highlight the terror inflicted there, so on it goes. I believed the death of Jill Dando was the best opportunity to highlight the plight of the Scottish nation because other murders could be connected to hers, but in the end her murder was conveniently solved when an innocent man was framed and the matter became a closed issue. It had been tough to live that way and be denied every opportunity just for domination of the English ruling classes. In the end I tried to make a difference but all that I did or achieved was professionally covered up and so it continued as before.

When Willie McCrae (the so-called Godfather of Scottish terrorism) was found dead in 1980 in the remote Scottish Highlands his 'suicide' and cause of death were always questioned. McCrae was the man that shot himself dead then supposedly threw the gun away three days later! A red Ford Escort is claimed to have left the scene at the time of his death suggesting there was more to the incident. A bungled police investigation followed with what appeared to be a deliberate obscuring of facts. The final anomaly was his business partner in his law practice in Glasgow disappeared immediately after this death. McCrae was not the only Glasgow lawyer to die in suspicious circumstances, another one, Jack Quar, also died suspiciously. You would think the legal profession in Scotland would start protesting at the deaths of their own.
In my opinion; the greatest protest they could make is to reinstate the law - have all those public officials guilty of wrong-

doing diving for cover with the threat of a prison sentence they so rightly deserve.

Was McCrae such a bad man? At the time of his death, stories circulated that he was planning to kidnap Princess Anne - this is the Queen's only daughter. What could be considered an ambitious stunt, was one that was destined to fail dramatically. Would he, as an intelligent man and a practicing lawyer, contemplate such a crime? Would he even be associated with such a foolhardy plan in any way? It is doubtful.
Was this story, which materialized after his death fabricated to disguise the truth? With a bungled police investigation leaving many to believe he was murdered and then the affair covered up, but, did all this hide a greater conspiracy? When I got a visit from the Men in Black, I did not believe justification came high on the list of priorities nor would any Government involvement be attached to it in the manner in which it was done. At the time of McCrae's death, he was said to be ecstatic where he held something over the British Government – not the behavior of a man about to commit suicide! Especially not with him in an ongoing struggle against the British Government. What did he have that was so important? A hair-brained plan to kidnap a Royal, as portrayed, with certain to be disastrous consequences, or something else; but, what could it have been?
McCrae, at the time of his death, was said to have held the evidence that an explosion had occurred at Dounrey Nuclear Power Station on the north coast of the country. The actual papers disclosing this could have possibly been the ones that were blown in the wind over the Highlands from where he fell. Twenty years later, amid repeated radioactive particles being found on the beach at Dounrey, details of the explosion were finally made public knowledge. In the meantime, a twenty year period, just how many unsuspecting people walked along that beach? How many of whom are suffering from cancers and other illnesses today? If not them, then deformities in their children. In the face of continued denial, there is no case for compensation for the victims, some of whom will already be deceased. Where, McCrae could have been murdered to make this possible! It is frightening to think this is the case, where not for the relatively

insignificant actions of his Commandos, but to potentially have so many people exposed to radiation could result in his silencing. The Clyde coast also has higher levels of cancer than other places; were the other nuclear power stations and the US military nuclear submarines responsible? We will never be able to ascertain an answer.

'We were heroes and victims of fate.'

11. THE CONCLUSION

'As a teenager my ambition at times was to get into town, the bright lights, where the action is, etc. Early one Saturday night, as a seventeen-year-old, I came down out the hills on my Raleigh Grifter bicycle but realized on approaching town there was nowhere to hide it, so I chose an appropriate thick bush, grabbed the bike by the seat and the handlebars then launched it into the middle of the foliage. At the end of the night the disco was finished and the beer was all gone but I remained sober unlike two of my three mates who were offering me a lift home. In the car, as it passed where the bicycle was hidden I beckoned to Graeham to stop the vehicle so I could retrieve it to cycle home. This would save me returning in the morning. Once I rescued the bike out of the vegetation, I was surprised to find the three of them were still waiting there.
"Give you a tow home," suggested one.
In a moment of wisdom to avoid the consequences of that one, I replied in low anticipation, "You don't have a tow rope."
In the end they coerced me into getting a tow without a rope; they would improvise. I vehemently stressed two conditions upon accepting this proposal; one, the car does not go above 15 MPH and two, when I asked to be released they would let go. No problem, this was all agreed, as Stuart in the passenger's seat wound down the window to face backwards so he could offer me his hand for the tow up the road. My left hand was on the left handlebar grip with my right forearm and elbow rested on the back passenger's side window of the Ford Cortina with Stuart now holding my right hand for this purpose. Off the car sped to a shaky start on a bicycle that was the forerunner of BMX bikes, which settled down to a comfortable ride up to 10 MPH, after which it developed a weave. At 15 MPH there was a profound speed wobble, then at 20 MPH the bicycle developed a violet

speed wobble but Stuart refused to let go and free me from this scary predicament. At 25 MPH the handlebars were flapping wildly full lock to full lock with no control whatsoever over the situation, but still the drunken idiot refused to let go. There is no description available for this when the car/bicycle combination hit 45 MPH. Handle-bars were going full lock one side to another hundreds of times a second, it simply defied the laws of physics how the bicycle remained upright, yet still the bold Stuart refused to free his grip. The single-track road was about to turn 45 degrees to the right, where all I could see straight ahead was a stone wall, sturdy with cement holding the stones in place. I am not one for taking the fear but at that particular moment and in this instance I was screaming, and still Stuart refused to let go. In the best comedy of the moment, Erik, drunk on the backseat decided to roll down the window and ask if I was OK. Was I OK? Two seconds before I was about to be pulverized into the stonework of that wall, screaming like a pig being roasted alive, in a situation that defied explanation and he asks if I am OK!

Moments like these could only happen to me; my forearm had been resting upon the window Erik just rolled down. I fell in towards the car, the bicycle shot out from below me and shot thirty-feet into the air such was the speed we were traveling at and, for one split second I was suspended in mid-air at the side of the car like a cartoon character. Was I OK?! The only thing that saves me in these situations is instinct as I thrust my upper-body away from the car and onto the grass verge and ditch only resulting in severe damage to both legs. Afterwards, I would swear God was sitting on that wall waiting for me. Maybe my time wasn't up, maybe it was planned I wasn't to die then but live on to tell another story – well, that's my conclusion.'

From the beginning, with that notorious class at Gateside Primary School where they openly told us we were the worst ever; maybe they were right. Teachers there never knew about incidents such as juvenile class-mates bringing in shotgun cartridges in an attempt to deliberately detonate them. We would huddle around in a circle behind the toilet block, hidden from staff quarters, where there was a slab of concrete on top of a cesspit with one of the little terrors throwing a cartridge as hard as he could at it in an attempt to detonate it. With a mixture of adrenaline and defiance tinged with fear we watched in anticipation where only the *unlucky* one died when it blew. All would obviously assure ourselves it wouldn't be me. Looking back in hindsight, in this case regarding how wrong we were: When a shotgun cartridge fires outside the gun it blows like a hand-grenade therefore would have killed us all. Had this happened the girl who rejected all others would then be alone in the class. She could then rightfully claim the trophy from those final exams.

All along I just thought the teachers told us we were the worst ever in the off chance we might behave ourselves...

PC H, and his type, were eradicated, where *intelligent* policeman did appear. We romanticize the past, where a certain camaraderie left society with him and his ilk. Do any of these supposedly clever officers drive down the streets of Glasgow, what was labeled the murder capital of Europe, or alternatively the heroine capital of Europe with the worst housing schemes and say, 'It was me, this is my doing, I helped create all this misery.'?

I doubt it.

They are that intelligent they couldn't see what they were part of, what they'd done, but the Queen of England would be quick to pin a medal on some of them so that made it acceptable...

Lessons learnt from Garnock Academy, teenage violence, defeatism instilled, would become paramount on guiding my situation and outlook in the overall scenario. Although I could see corruption on the surface then, it was a lot worse than expected once fully experienced. Truth is, there is no justice system, no democracy, a corrupt evil regime totalitarian in nature with no way out for the aggrieved. Scotland is probably the worst example of a police state in the Western world yet propaganda says differently.

On fighting against odds that, quite frankly, were never odds but more akin to insanity. I could never see it then but only now on a higher level where it did and does have a bearing. I, for one, recall all the lives I saved when Government agents wanted to allegedly murder everybody in Strathclyde solely to get at oil reserves in the Clyde Estuary - propaganda denies it is there, plus a Labour politician produced similar deceptive statements.

In the end, I got fed up having to cover-up for others, always keeping quiet, always looking silly so some bag-of-wind could pretend what a big man he was. I knew if they ever once had to go out and do the job they would never bullshit again. It was so easy telling them that had produced the goods, and those that dreamed about it, and I don't mean because the majority of protagonists were now invariably suffering psychological problems - drug addiction and alcoholism being two sure symptoms of the unfortunate few. Maybe the cause they once fought for wasn't all it was cracked up to be in later life. Maybe the hell they'd been through was just too much. The ones who'd done the job knew me and I recognised them.
An example of this was the drunken Orangeman proudly boasting one night "*WE* never bombed, *WE* shoot people."
It was obvious upon hearing such he never had to point a gun at anyone, never mind pull the trigger. The day he has to, it will no longer be a proud boast to him; the stench of death is sickening devoid of romance. Only the real hard bastards and psychopaths can do it and live with themselves afterwards without psychological problems - maybe they have them to begin with so it fitted right in with their personality. When he said *WE* he was associating himself with the whole British Loyalist movement.
Such a deranged boast could be disputed with alleged involvement of Loyalist terrorists in the bombings of Dublin and Monaghan in the 1970s.

When I was fifteen, a friend hurt me badly which at a young age was difficult to accept destroying my faith in human nature. Years later, there he was driving his small van up the single-track road towards my home with me driving down in the opposite direction. We stopped to talk face-to-face like we did often since those early times. He was in a dreadful state. Soaking wet, and reminded me of a baby, both crying and sucking onto a massive bottle of whiskey in the same way an infant would onto its mother's breast. I asked what was wrong; him having to physically wipe away tears before answering. The reply could have been predicted in the circumstances, when saying he was about to commit suicide. With someone in this state there is no saving them. This is not *Hollywood*, where you talk them out of it, tell them life is wonderful, that they have it all to live for, for this is real life and it becomes brutal at times.

The reason he was wet was because he'd been at the local quarry face further up this road standing there for hours in the pouring rain looking over the edge contemplating jumping. Unable to complete the act he went for a bottle of whiskey to give himself Dutch courage. I heard the truth about his situation sitting there sharing a last drink. No, this is not *Hollywood* and I had to tell him the truth sitting there saying to end it. Reality can be a cruel beast. There was no saving him. I amaze myself at times, for I produced miracles that night to keep him alive and when the moment was right I raced away leaving him with the decision to either kill himself or to turn his van around and follow me into town. At a distance I looked in the interior mirror to see his van following; I'd pulled off the impossible again.

The bottle of whiskey we shared was the biggest available. Still the situation went on, for he had nowhere to sleep that night. So the two of us went in search of his sister. I was now driving his van with him in the passenger seat lapsing in and out of conscience, but I needed to keep him awake because he could see the road and I couldn't with the steamed up interior. With the amount of whiskey downed to keep him company in what should have been his final hour my eyes glazed up in drunkenness thereby he became the navigator, as we raced into the rain and darkness blind, with him periodically shouting "Turn now; no turn now."

With the van hitting off grass verges at the sides of the road, I knew we could never stop as I rammed other vehicles off the roads and past the traffic police car racing in the opposite direction – were they after us?! On left-hand corners he would land on top of me such was the centrifugal force, as I fought to control the vehicle and remove his bulk from the gear-stick and handbrake. We raced around the countryside unable to find his sister until she was finally located at a friend's house.

I burst in the front door to a startled audience who presumed I was in trouble. These were troubled times where such an assumption was understandable. Unable to comprehend what I was trying to relay due drunkenness someone finally ventured outside to find my companion lying unconscious in the garden. I'd entered the house thinking he'd followed. Once the situation calmed down and those present worked out roughly what had happened from meager bits of information transmitted or demonstrated, the three of us made for their parents' house.

There I was sitting on the settee laughing at the moon, crazed on whiskey and adrenaline, with his mother having no one to blame for the situation, so obviously it was all my fault that her boy had hit the skids?! What the woman failed to recognize was my clothes were dry unlike his, for he was both soaked to the skin and covered in dirt from the garden. Had she acknowledged this, maybe she would have realized there was more to the situation. I couldn't tell the woman there was two potential situations; the one in hand or she could be in the morgue right now identifying her son. Instead of any gratitude I sat there listening to insults. It was only later did I find out his so-called best friend gave him that bar-sized bottle to kill himself. On hearing this I asked myself; why didn't I just let him die?

I looked in the mirror three days later, unable to recognize the reflection. A hand got raised to remove what I thought was a superimposed image on the glass only to realize it was my hand and this was my face; the experience was too much. Years of torment then this; never again. I didn't need it any more. I'd nothing left to prove to anyone. I had saved his life and that of so many others, only to be left asking myself, for what? Insults? Poverty? Humiliation? Isolation? There certainly was never any gratitude?!

Afterwards, his family called around the countryside to thank and apologize to them involved that night, with one exception - myself. A couple of months later his other sister took me aside saying he was off the rails again, where if I found him, could I do something again. I had already promised myself, no more, the next time I would watch him die with no remorse, no regrets, and a totally clear conscience. I had had enough.

I questioned many aspects of that incident. Like, why I was now saving the life of someone who hurt me in the past, or the fact it is his so called best friend that helps kill him yet I was the one to rectify the situation. I simply could not justify what I'd done; I didn't want to be a hero. The bullshit continued, but I knew it made no difference if he had any last minute regrets, for in disrepair he only needed to go to the quarry face and would have fell over the lip. Whiskey would have taken him over like it did for him in the van or in the garden. The truth is there was no one else to save him but I would have to hear all them tell me different afterwards. There was no thanks for what I'd done only insults and an expectation I would be there the next time to do it again. I never told his sister how I felt. How could you? So in the end I just let it pass like every other impossible situation experienced. All I ever truly acknowledged from this episode was the pressure certainly does take its toll!

After this episode, Glasgow had a spate of potential suicides, with men about to jump into the River Clyde from the bridges spanning the city center only to be talked down by 'hero' policemen. Either the Glaswegians got fed up with the number of these antics or never believed such attempts were real, as they encouraged them to jump but of course they never did suggesting it was all staged. All were done in full public view in broad daylight, whereas if these were genuine this would not be the case. The last thing a dying person wants is the full gaze of publicity to complete their humiliating circumstances. Glaswegians are a hard bunch to fool at times, with this seen as a circus act, not the final moments in someone's life. Was this a copy of my actions, which were authentic, being staged to promote what a wonderful police force is operating? It is fitting with the pathetic mentality they possess. Could they not demonstrate how wonderful they are by providing the service they are paid for for once?

The greatest reflection is from the gist of this short story to the larger scenario I found myself in - although with the last paragraph it is possible they were intertwined. Scots were doing it to themselves. Every little betrayal to assist the authorities in their evil agenda done as gestures of goodwill by public spirited people was fueling the prevailing scenario. Every time Scots Law failed to provide justice was to ensure democracy never returned. Every crime that went unpunished because it was done by a Unionist politician, policeman or a member of the Secret Service exacerbated the situation. Every media story pumped out like a propaganda service cost more lives.

In *2. Case Study*, for by being biologically poisoned with a rapidly developing culture from a virus in the milk I have been chemically poisoned with blue chemicals in the water, crop-sprayed with a dirty dust that possessed a bad odor plus chemtrails with clear gelatin like blobs with a green nuclei in the center similar in structure to that of a tadpole, and, I can even claim to have been gassed by this evil Jewish influenced regime yet no Jew, that I ever got to know of, was ever gassed by Germans in World War Two!

Who was offering to hack into the FEDs? Glaswegian Gary MicKinnon, then living in England, was arrested for it. Whether he was the source or not I honestly don't know for it was through a third party, but I vehemently stressed them not to it! The Americans wanted him extradited but his mother fought the case citing he suffered from Asbergers syndrome. Popular opinion said they only want him there to join the NSA to hack into members of the public...

One British soldier present at Bloody Sunday did have a pair of balls. He refused to fire upon unarmed civilians when under orders to - in difference to what the official inquiries state - and was thrown out the British Army for it! I met him in the past. Likewise, at Gibraltar when three IRA suspects were murdered by the SAS, one former member told me they were unarmed wearing summer clothes, making their circumstances over obvious, yet lies told at the time said differently.

Convicted killer Levi Bellfield was targeted in a corrupt manner for the double murder of Lin and Megan Russell where the press portrayed him as being guilty prior to going on trial - he never did stand trial - when it is well known who the actual killer is yet he is never arrested?! All of which occurred with someone else in prison for it at the time demonstrating it was all a circus convicting who they like yet letting the pedophile killer run free...

My troublesome brother later fled to the south island of New Zealand, whereon a couple met him who then later reported they felt he was running away from something - my reply being reality.

In *3. Strategy,* what is not said is a single attack or incident is never enough for it will be contained or manipulated by the authorities to an extent it will disappear from public conscientiousness - referring back to them having full control over the media. It is best to complicate the matter to get a credible result, where this needs to be done in such a manner outside of the authorities' control. Likewise, you have to wait until their first response materializes so to complicate the overall scenario in a method of exposing treachery comprising what is being done to cover up their initial actions - basically wait until they lie about the situation before revealing your full hand. Ultimately, I was playing them at their own game and winning for I honestly never had a prayer. It was they who provided all the targets, where I set them up then had them knock their own out! The events regarding David Gilles fully illustrates the above, when I only wanted him to appear in court...

In regards to the banking industry for guidance; American Timothy Geithner was hailed a hero for partially proposing the solution to Europe's debt crisis. I could see from day one what needed doing, which was an extension of what he proposed: Germany, on being the strongest and largest country within the EU, should borrow all monies required to service Euro currency countries' debts. It borrows at, say, one percent interest then lends that money out to other countries at, say, two percent interest, where with such large sums involved a massive reserve fund quickly builds up from the surplus one percent made on every transaction to then be used to bail out any failing EU country. I was never any *master of the universe* - maybe that should read pompous twat - but I seen it so clearly such is the utter simplicity of banking!

Returning to discuss diagnosing the manipulation of my foolish brother; he was taken down to London for a few days on request of his suspect girlfriend where after it became obvious he was being mind-controlled! It was being triggered over the telephone. If you lifted the receiver when it rang when meant for him, there would be burbs peeps whistles and squeaks, which was obviously a means of triggering. I remember one instance in particular with the phone ringing, he briefly answered then on putting down the receiver instantly turned on me for no apparent reason when I was laid-back not involved in the general social scene present. What happened on the telephone set him off, yet it was in mere seconds, corresponding with the chirps and squeaks being brief. My guess is he was taken to Tavistock Institute London for this conditioning!

The double murder of Lin and Megan Russell has a few facts remaining awkward. A broad-shouldered killer with light hair was sought before the details changed upon corrupting the evidence and investigation. Dr Shaun Russell matched this description but the police claimed to have CCTV footage he was elsewhere at the time of the double murder, which does not explain why his DNA was found at the crime scene. Another police statement contradicted the first when claiming to have other CCTV images of him at another location at the relevant time. He could not be in three different locations at once, so, where was he when his family were butchered? Another question; what is his actual relationship to the British Establishment?

Above child murder and another in Scotland pertaining to the removal of a Scottish Police Chief is exactly how the British authorities operate - such a statement will cause shock and disbelief to some readers. They know emotions are distorted so abuse the situation to their advantage. You wondered just how low these people go, well now you know! Alternatively, you can watch an internet video allegedly of Hillary Clinton in a snuff movie to get a fuller picture of what I am really up against - for all them that sided with such evil they should be forced to watch this obscenity.

Porton Down is mentioned here where all the chemical and biological agents being used to poison unsuspecting civilians had to materialize from somewhere?! At the time of the *Novichok* poisonings in England; once it was exposed Russia had little or no potential for such an act with the finger of suspicion shifting back to British State agents, in particular when the Russians pointed out the victims having not immediately died from such thereby an antidote had to be administered to keep them alive therefore them that held it were most likely the culprits. A Scottish spokesman from Porton Down appeared on television making a comment about they only develop biological agents for defense; such does not explain how people in Scotland are being killed by such when British agents, again, remain the only suspects?! What he said could be similar to the misleading MI5 statement, such like, they kill nobody - this is technically correct for they issue a brief to the SAS to carry out such assassinations.

On leaving Scotland: For a while I never wanted to depart in a hasty manner for such could be made appear that I was fleeing as a fugitive for the murder of Tracey Wilde. It didn't matter I had proven beyond doubt Raymond Stevenson killed her and planted my DNA at the murder scene, With a law as corrupt as it is I could still have been wrongfully convicted. My actual calling card to leave was when my sister returned from abroad with a new boyfriend, where upon knowing I knew some of life's characters, asked if I could get him something to smoke. That night I could have potentially went to six different smugglers and bought a ton of cannabis from each though never honestly knew who the local drug dealer is?! The penny dropped there and then. This life had become too fucked up for words! I had to get out.

All along I'd been playing at a higher level alienated from my family and most friends partially due to State agent manipulation of the brother previously mentioned. From a wretched messed-up existence, bankrupt, plus living under virtual house arrest yet with the regular occurrence of hitmen – State and gangland – being allowed to operate with impunity against me. Upon leaving in these circumstances it provided resuscitation.

The war fought was dark. I could not see the light at the end of the tunnel. At times I could not see tomorrow such were the dire circumstances where that is a dangerous scenario to be in, but today I can see it all in the broader picture. I suffered so others could live. Utter scumbag types who opposed me and inflicted such horror onto so many innocent people will have to live with themselves today; can they? A majority of whom on the front-line were Scottish men, whereas in my support the majority of whom were international women, probably due to them feeling vulnerable where it could spread to include them next!

In 2006, after having spent four and a half months on the run with two different death squads and over forty personnel on the ground, plus many others behind the scenes (probably totaling over a hundred!), I shockingly found a local battalion of the Provisionals put me on a death-list in the middle of which?! This threat independent of the cover-story British authorities spread about to reduce suspicion upon death when a friend elsewhere said I was on an IRA hit-list. He never got access to other IRA information prior to this upon not possessing those contacts. I was the victim of a local mistake that was not trans-national, so his source has to be British Intelligence related to cover their actions (if successful), and not localized Irish nonsense.

My opinion of the Provisional IRA plummeted right there and then. This was, in my opinion, just a group of silly little boys trying to play big boys' games, otherwise it would never have happened. Did they not see SAS members such as David Gilles, Sgt Tom Kennedy, or Martin Jones' replacement, British Special Branch operating on Irish soil, where the guns were physically on the streets at times with the risk of arrest that entails, MI5 officers present with no interest in any local, a surveillance network in operation and fully functional etc, etc, all acutely focusing upon me as their distinct target?! Local rednecks certainly never acknowledged my status. For it is only a world ranking that could rise from here - I was certainly in the top one hundred, maybe even in the top ten, most dangerous men in this world! The situation got worst. In simple terms, the local IRA attempted to cause me grief but lacked the necessary bottle to carry it out?! All those big hard terrorists up against a small ostracized person struggling to just stay alive running raggedly from post to post - at the time thee most vulnerable person in Ireland therefore the easiest possible target they could pick upon.

In the end, with the British death squad then absent, I got fed up waiting to be shot by the IRA so decided to be more proactive. The devil inside was obviously acting up, or maybe it was just plain curiosity regarding their capabilities (or lack of?)… There was this one little character that would suck up to all Provos he could find. To be honest, there was no evidence to say he was actually a member, but it became irrelevant, he was attempting to cause me the most aggravation when most vulnerable – it is like living with both hands tied behind your back where no matter how badly you are insulted or by whom there is no alternative but to take it in silence. That said, force of habit meant I always pick one out later as an example to return the favor… First come, first served, where he happened to be there... From his outlook, his actions meant a protection racket was in place therefore believed he was untouchable. However, this reckoning possessed a simple flaw; this idiot was trying to pull this nonsense off against the wrong person. When up against them, knowing what they really are and with my dastardly situation relieved a little (although still precarious); did I really care if there were twenty of them? Not really; I would smack the worst problem first then deal with the next one until the full nineteen were dealt with, one way or another, even if it took me ten years to do so if I so desired. To be honest, I was plain fed up waiting for bull-shitters to act so a little incentive, such as a broken nose, would be appropriate. When I found their annoying associate alone one day without his henchmen (exaggerating their status here), well, I wasn't about to miss the opportunity so lunged at him. He recoiled. He broke down into a little girl squealing, "I'll call the cops on you."

Surprise; surprise; this was an informer. A pathetic little rat playing a double game but caught out badly here. And; what was it the local IRA were accusing me of? You guessed it, of being an informer. Deranged hypocrites that they are. My only response to which was to curiously ask them, "On what?"

This was always met with a blank expression devoid of verbal reply, probably due to them not having one. Alternatively, they quoted words and phrases from *Hollywood* 1920s gangster movies. From knowing how gangland really operates, I have to say it was highly embarrassing reaching new lows of stupidity and depravity every time. There was no explaining I probably knew some of the most dangerous men and women in the world (likewise they would have known me) yet not one of them ever held an accusation against me. For I was (for an expression) playing with the big boys, to be lied about threatened and insulted by these pathetic rats relying upon group security?! The situation defied comprehension.

I have always been the victim of informers so honestly never knew who or what I was supposed to inform on (and certainly knew of a lot more capable characters than these fools), or how to go about it?!

I never got to punch their member friend accomplice lover or whatever he is, he was just too pathetic to give a good smack. On retreat without assault I turned on a heel to shockingly find myself face-to-face with an Irish policewoman. Luck was never my best friend when now facing arrest… Intuition is a fine thing. I pointed back at this informer when faced with this slightly taller woman to announce; "A rat."

Instead of doing her duty and slapping a pair of handcuffs on the wrists, reading me my rites, doing the frog-march up to a police cell etc, she bewilderingly nodded in agreement with a pleasant smile of acknowledgment?! These reactions giving further confirmation of his status, in light of fact police officers are prohibited from giving out such information.

In reflection, she (shockingly) held a decency to her upon being unable to stomach the low-life characters dealt with every day. Whereas he just found out his police protection deserted him at the first instance and the big bad bhoys from the IRA he would go running to held no fear factor for me whatsoever, hence, corresponding with which, nonexistent reprisals!

For a long time I'd been contemplating the Provisionals being little boys living in a big boys' world – them shitting themselves when about to hand over a shotgun yet I was unfazed when only two hours away from dying fighting the SAS with such a useless weapon – them saving the life of an SAS member when not having the *rag-dolls* to fight them (had I revealed his true status) – them not acknowledging I was under constant surveillance and attack by British agents – them bull-shitting then believing the excrement talked - them putting a bewildered person (me) on a fantasy death-list then not pulling the trigger – them having the ultimate target of an SAS sergeant driving around in his jeep like royalty (he was also driver to other high profile targets) presented before them but lacking the guts to attack him and would only hinder me if I decided to - them being accused of having so many informers in their ranks (another one suspected was no longer seen locally) – them being so clueless yet pretending to be a force worth reckoning with – them standing up for pedophiles (and having such allegations against individual members) - them being fooled by this cling-on – I did ask myself; were they getting blow-jobs from him? For, I couldn't guess at the overall relationship between them. Now I was laughing on the inside at what in essence was a freak-show but not about to reveal the truth. It couldn't get any more corrupt debauched or embarrassing, but for certain it did… and then more so…

To give a realistic inclination pertaining to the level of this faction; a young lad said how they operate. As a fifteen-years-old he was stealing cars. The Provisionals knew this so tried to use it to their advantage asking him to murder somebody on their behalf as part of a let-off deal. What he was asked to do was to crash a car into the victim. Then get out of the wreckage and slit the other driver's throat. They gave him the knife but no mention of money or any decent pay-off for the deed. Thankfully, he refused, for he would be left with this on his conscience for his remaining days had he not been strong enough as resist what they couldn't carry out themselves! I live by simple rules; you never ask someone to do what you are not capable of yourself. Likewise, when in serious trouble offers come your way... They should learn that!

To continue: Glasgow gangster Frank Ward appeared this night in the pub. Not initially knowing who it was, Frank, not being the shy retiring type, told locals unceremoniously his opinions on them (with me cringing in agreement knowing he was telling them a few home truths). One little wise-guy against thirty locals on home turf, such odds were not favorable. Not that he was about to let this disadvantage hinder proceedings. A small commotion caused the bar owner to be seen talking on the telephone. Doors at the front locked and chained shut mysteriously had a local IRA member appear through them like a ghost (or a guest). His first action was to find a new best friend that night. A very awkward one, for it was an undercover police officer. No shame to him standing there shoulder-to-shoulder like bosom buddies. Upon seeing this I had to think quickly; either tell Frank what the situation really was, with terminally grave doubts he would acknowledge it given he was a stranger here and with him getting into his stride, or, depart hoping he would pipe down a little? I left knowing this to be the only realistic option. To conclude the story; that mobster would be found dead thirty-six hours later upon return to Glasgow. I was livid, for that same IRA man mouthed off most telling all before him I was a grass or a rat or whatever, when he was one of them that would go dumbstruck when I bewilderingly asked, "On what?"

The IRA has stated rules where predominant among which is no informing. After what happened I openly said what these people really were, "Rats", until I was asked not to with, "You can't go around calling the Provos rats."

For once, it was said without malice, as is their deluded form thinking they can threaten whoever they please when lacking the muscle to enforce it. Had it not been said in such a manner it is doubtful I would have listened…

I even offered to go to Glasgow to tell Frank Ward's gang members exactly what happened that night to let them sort it out billing any forthcoming battle as the, 'Rats against the gangsters'. Again, local IRA members backed down, though an IRA man from elsewhere asked me to...

Afterwards, I left the vicinity to live elsewhere in Ireland repulsed and cringing in embarrassment at how these informers with their lies had turned so many people against me, did me every injustice imaginable, worked their utmost to ruin my life when I endured abysmal conditions to begin with, yet I never once did them an injustice having always planned to keep them at arms' length from knowing their reputation for informing. Where all of this was combined with a shocking level of child abuse this neighborhood is infamous for (in two different parts of town you could hear children regularly screaming at night) – not that this IRA gang were about to resolve this issue either with such allegations leveled against individual members! A personal embarrassment these people were the likes of which you couldn't comprehend yet devious enough to retain local support here in *Kiddiefilingville*!

Elsewhere in the south of Ireland, a second accommodation in this new neighborhood would make me close neighbors with who is the alleged overall leader of what should long have been the defunct Provisional IRA. He knew who I was prior to meeting him, and possessed an awkward fascination. A former flat-mate constantly brought his name up with sentences I featured in when wishing he didn't. This leader was said to live with his sister, was probably around fifty years old, and, from inside sources claimed he was gay. If true, this is a weird science when Provisionals are said to avoid homosexuals?! Other than once announcing 'Robert', I suppose to check for facial recognition, to which I never replied, there was no contact between us. Much later, his only other single word response was to call me a, "Wanker."

At the time this felt rather strange given I have a stunning girlfriend, with him not seen in the arms of neither men nor women! Obsessed, constantly interested in me, making insinuating comments, such a weird obsession was always going to culminate in the most bizarre conclusion...

The following is going to sound absurd; for it took me months to realize what he actually did. It is best to understand I strive night and day to find a little cash just to stay alive with a constant death threat hanging over me. Few people will ever relate to such circumstances, where you are blind to day-to-day living others are engrossed in, yet they think otherwise, likewise such an assumption increases my vulnerability.

After a period he changed homes. Such a move may have been instrumental to his forthcoming plans. Rumors started circulating I was a pedophile?! The source of these lies were this peculiar character. Now any decent person would be questioning him and his personal circumstances, but with a small army to command to help spread false propaganda they bizarrely accepted these falsehoods?! Further, they were also spreading rumors I was stealing bicycles. I had taken parts off of bicycles with council tags on them to indicate they were going to the dump, nothing more; i.e. some recycling.

A guess to why he was behaving like this was my rejection – though no approach was made – to fight for them?! I honestly had no interest in for I was getting older. I'd spent decades on the run. I was now a family man; whence with, the only thing I really craved was a normal life at this point in time – something the IRA worked tirelessly to deny me. This meant not to be part of some phony war for untrustworthy people with the increasing levels of embarrassment they were. Alternatively, I could single-handedly pull off more victories against the British State than what they could collectively. Of the ten percent of attacks I credit the Provisional IRA of achieving on their own two feet without any outside British assistance, this is probably as low as five percent such is the level of ineptitude, thereby it could just be resentment on their behalf, hence this leads to me being under constant attack?!

When I viewed certain factions of the Provisional IRA being little boys wanting to play big boys' games I obviously overrated them. Little girls bitching in a school playground possessed more dignity than some of them. They took me, probably the only person in Ireland with a restraining order out against them for attacking Irish pedophiles, and attempted to make this nonsense stick. This being the same population with a pressure group called *1 in 4*, for that is the percentage abused as children. A prominent Irish judge allegedly caught with pedophile porn on his computer. Plus; the same Irish known the world over as pedophiles, irrespective to whether they are or not such is their depraved behavior. For once, I remained unfazed because it was strikingly obvious where this was heading – a public outcry against those involved once the truth emerges, for he never possessed the foresight to check my details prior to lying. Further, this will be found an affront to many of his number given all of the suffering and loss individual members experienced in the past at the hands of the British authorities. I only ever knew a meager few Irish to address their national depravity, but thankfully this number is growing because Ireland is a changing country, where with it some will finally muster the courage to tell the Provisional IRA there is a law of the jungle: You do such an act once - where they did - and it is unforgivable and unforgettable. Life has certain golden rules which nobody should transgress.

As for me upon writing this and not being prepared to sacrifice the safety of a single child in disregard towards my personal safety; will they circle the wagons, close ranks like a mafia, just like they did with their informing, to have me under attack once again? Only, in this instance such a strategy maybe too late for them…

In life, it all comes full circle; in Scotland it was originally a former IRA family of informers and pedophiles that caused all the grief for me!

Supposed IRA murder of Lord Mountbatten?! It was only in the press did it really get blamed upon the Provisional IRA, yet they, in my opinion, lacked the skill-set to pull off such a feat! A supposed bomb-maker, McMahon, was convicted of his murder (and of others who died with him), yet it is said he was framed. It was an entirely one-off hit of outstanding magnitude. Locally, I once heard a bizarre claim that, *'Mountbatten was killed by British forces because he was a pedophile?!'*

The only other high profile Royal murder in recent times being Princess Diana where her bodyguard, Trevor Ryhs-Jones, later

admitted carrying out her execution. Of all the information and stories – true or false - to transpire from that car crash the only detail missing is Trevor's status; he was in fact SAS – that came from inside sources!
Now, the Royal family has allegations against individual members for abusing children and so many within the British Establishment are accused of such. At the time of Thatcher there were allegations she was surrounded by pedophiles! One after another, only upon death to prevent conviction and further exposure, evidence and witnesses emerged (or were they finally allowed to speak out) to support these claims. It was the death of Jimmy Saville that opened this scrutiny up with further allegations he was not only involved in abusing children but supplying them to friends in high places. He shared Government and Royal connections?! Sir Peter Morrison and Sir Lion Britan were close to Thatcher where allegations surrounded them in the 1980s about child abuse, but, as said, only upon death did such question marks become prevalent. All of which brings us back to Mountbatten. Prince Charles was always said to be *close,* with their relationship having a certain bond to it; what was being referred to by this?

In general, Irish gangsters also reject the Provisional IRA for allies, but will form allegiances with the INLA mainly for weapons supply.

In conclusion, I once believed the perceived hyped status of the Provisional IRA, but they were in fact very localized only being in control of certain neighborhoods, where, in general, they lacked the foresight to do anything substantial away from which - a situation that (wrongfully) leads them to attacking who is closest to them. It was them who came to believe British propaganda about their levels of expertise and threat. Individually, they relied upon group security (although there were around fifteen of them that could be respected for they were capable of fighting the SAS) where it was strength in numbers, but this was also a weakness with so many informers recruited or turned, and, from a personal perspective, I never knew them to be capable of anything other than wrongfully attempt (and fail) to control other people's lives.

Now for the conspiracy theory – its been a while in the making... We have the Provisional IRA, as I viewed them only capable of limited acts. Nothing more! Their actions were mostly localized. Rarely international! A total of around three thousand members past and present meant there was increased numbers informers within them. Reducing their capabilities! An overall leader capable of pulling off what amounts to tittle-tattle. Little more that I know of! A success rate (kill rate) that was very low. At best! So what if the British authorities needed to up their capabilities to justify their existence and expense? British informers fed into IRA cells were allowed to kill with impunity - this is well documented. Likewise, informers turned when already being inside such cells (a superior method of infiltration) were also allowed to kill with impunity. Both scenarios were done to place informers above suspicion. In the process it increased the supposed kill rate of the Provos. That's undeniable! Likewise, when the SAS operated there (forget that nonsense about they only fire when fired upon) they were told to, 'Shoot the cunts' in situations when RUC police officers got in the way - that exact phrase is repeated coming from different SAS sources. Cover-up operations with incidents carried out by the SAS generally had the onus wrongfully placed upon the IRA. At Omagh in 1998 when a terrorist bomb killed 28 innocent civilians I was (disbelievingly) told the SAS were responsible! At the time I thought this was being said as Real IRA propaganda due to school children being murdered, but incident after incident supported this horrendous claim! Regrettably, informers and SAS were killing British personnel in Ireland at an alarming rate. On hindsight, that's undeniable. Where this is going is to suggest the entire show was a phony war orchestrated from above?! The phrase, fog of war, is a good one. When on the front-line, this is your absolute focus, you couldn't care a jot about anything else nor likely to see it then. Only when you look in hindsight does the full picture emerge with altered perceptions, especially so when supplied with differing accounts and more accurate up-to-date information.

The American version of this conspiracy theory centers on their terrorist enemy of ISIS. It is alleged ISIS were armed by Americans, then allegedly allowed a free reign to attack. Images of their convoys being attacked by American airstrikes is allegedly false. Russians were fighting an honest war - if such ever existed. For it was they who would attack these ISIS convoys. Allegedly, the Americans forces then hacked into on-board footage of such attacks to then take the footage back to the United States to be broadcast in mainstream media as US strikes against *their* enemy?!

In reference to *4. Publicity and Propaganda* when I attacked the SAS in 2008, where after, I would never have said a word about it as was my practice, but the IRA now had knowledge of what I was capable of – what they dreamed of doing but could never pull it off. With which, I became infamous for this, combined with a sensationalized inclusion in a national tabloid newspaper article associating me with dissident Republicans, which I never was. With no interest I never read the nonsense printed.

To have been privy to Libya's State secrets, the same source maintained the murder of PC Yvonne Flechter near the Libyan embassy in London was not their doing, for it was impossible for the accused to have made such a shot…

From what I consistently found one attack was never sufficient to remove or dispose of an enemy when manipulating the system to my advantage, like I did in chapter *5. The Greatest Act*, for British State agents have outright control over all matters concerning them. I had to take it outside this sphere of control and provide a secondary front to get a credible result. This was done by manipulating Irish policing and Intelligence so there was an unknown factor – one the British couldn't readily control. Ultimately, it was, on my behalf, a test of democracy, but obviously that doesn't exist within the British State, for them responsible for Gilles' murder were never tried for treason.

Sebastion Morley was an untouchable given his previous position to point out such details.

In *6. Questionable Motives* where is says the SAS live like low-life characters unable to justify their actions; it went a lot deeper than that. With Thatcher, from the claim she was surrounded with pedophiles, it is the SAS who help protect the guilty and know the truth.

If the British State were 'preparing the ground' for an oil boom in the Clyde Estuary it has yet to happen, instead the next boom has unexpectedly begun in the Shetland Isles…

For *7. Laws and Rules* all I state is it does come full circle.

8. Politics.

9. Authorities have for years possessed absolute control (ex-NSA Edward Snowden confirmed this), therefore they could never afford to have it challenged in any manner. Any loss of power irks them tremendously because from it the scenario could cascade down upon them to give people hope of achieving results where this perceived threat is what I utilize to get results?!

10. Characters I never was and never wanted to be included here where I questioned the status obtained upon being too meek to deserve it. My only claims were that I knew (now long in the past) the hard-men and gangsters in society, but steadfastly maintained I was never one of them. Only a fool claims to be included there when they are not. For unlike certain members of the Provisional IRA, you have to earn respect the hard way and never lose face once granted, which means doing dastardly heroic acts. In a circuitous manner I did become one of life's characters! Further, like most of them, in a circuitous manner I became fucked-up on it where it became difficult to be anything other...

I was also probably being manipulated to justify the ever increasing Security budget the British tax-payer has to forfeit with no say in the matter when falsely claiming there are nasty people out there about to attack them. I never once did anything I wasn't forced into, thereby it is a security services that creates the terrorist to justify their expense and very existence! For by saving countless lives to their annoyance, I also used up their manpower budget and resources to make it more difficult for them to assault others at the same time.

My father once said I needed to learn to fight my own battles! He never honestly knew I had taken on and defeated more members of the SAS than anybody else in this world, such is the void in which I operate!

A conclusion on *11. Conclusion.* I never wanted to go down this route pinning the blame on an individual family, but only when writing here did the full picture of the Rotheschild family emerge with their impact upon the situation. From early beginnings of being Jewish conmen - they tried to ban a book portraying the family in an honest manner - they became the world's bankers and richest family. Corresponding with this, a pattern exists of removing Jewish involvement in human rights violations in recent history from Jews being involved in the slave trade onwards. The State of Israel being a pet project for this family, where, from inside sources Shin Bet - lesser known intelligence sister organization to Mossad - admit behind closed doors there was no holocaust in World War II! No surprise there then with a supposed six million dead Jews nobody can find the remains of, or, then to be told they cremated them when it is impossible to do so with such a volume of corpses, and, with me being old enough to remember the old people who did fight in the War scoffing at how badly the Jews were supposedly treated when they liberated them only to be insulted (and jailed) for telling the truth about it, and Glasgow giving the greatest percentage of men to fight when being deceived. Alternatively, Freemasons were also a target group for the Nazis, but never once do they claim a holocaust when suffering the same wartime fate as the Jews. All of which leaves us today with wrongful sympathy for Jews. They then abuse this ill situation to their advantage.

Scotland's premier broadsheet newspaper, *The Scotsman,* (although the readership and quality of content declined in recent years) is Rotheschild owned, this I only realized when it went up for sale with them pulling assets out of the United Kingdom. Rotheschild family members are an intricate part of the British Secret Service - no matter what deceit is produced to disguise the fact - and in the Russian spy rings to emerge of Blunt Burgess McLean Cairncross and Philby the sixth man that was never found, or continues to be covered up, was alleged to be the head of MI6, a Rotheschild! I know family involvement in the British Secret Service continues into present times.

Finally, to complete the picture, who is alleged to be the world's only trillionaire, Jacob Rotheschild, is on record boasting how much money he makes from Scotland's North Sea oil reserves.

So here you have it, at face value the Rotheschild family would not just appear to be a stain on humanity but an active force to prevent humanity developing. The adage about Jews enslaving humanity could hold water. I could have done so much to improve the quality of life of others, instead of temporary halting a British State murder campaign where all the aspects are still in position for it to resume. Through the worst of it, I was continually confronted with the phrase New World Order in connection to events, but I never knew the meaning of such. Only now do I read this allegedly refers to Zionist Jews wanting to massacre ninety percent of the world's population! If that is true, I suppose they had to start somewhere. Scotland really is at the end of the line. The United States can bully and cajole England into doing its bidding, where England dominates this corrupt Union, so once the law is stamped out, which it is as demonstrated firsthand, subservient police officers are in place to create a police state, which has happened, and then the slaughter can begin, exactly as it occurred with the laughable free press there to tell those living there what a wonderful deal they are getting!

Once liberated, Scotland has enormous potential where a spin-off from which could benefit the north of England, which in turn could level out the disparity of England being rich in the south and poor in the north, instead of the elites running off with all the wealth and the Rotheschild family having the nation as a practical fiefdom to nobody's benefit other than their own.

'Nae mair yer bonnie callants gang tae war.'

CPSIA information can be obtained
at www.ICGtesting.com
Printed in the USA
LVHW091545071218
599652LV00003B/526/P